# CHAMONIX MOUNTAIN
# ADVENTURES

# CHAMONIX MOUNTAIN ADVENTURES

## by Hilary Sharp

CICERONE

JUNIPER HOUSE, MURLEY MOSS,
OXENHOLME ROAD, KENDAL, CUMBRIA LA9 7RL
www.cicerone.co.uk

© Hilary Sharp 2012
First edition 2012
ISBN 978 1 85284 663 3
Reprinted (with updates) 2013, 2016, 2022

Printed in India by Replika Press Pvt Ltd using responsibly sourced paper.
A catalogue record for this book is available from the British Library.
All photos are by Hilary Sharp or Jon de Montjoye unless otherwise stated.

### Dedication

*To my bike, garden, cat and husband, all much
neglected in the frantic final stages.*

### Updates to this Guide

While every effort is made by our authors to ensure the accuracy of
guidebooks as they go to print, changes can occur during the lifetime of an
edition. Any updates that we know of for this guide will be on the Cicerone
website (www.cicerone.co.uk/663/updates), so please check before
planning your trip. We also advise that you check information about such
things as transport, accommodation and shops locally. Even rights of way
can be altered over time. We are always grateful for information about any
discrepancies between a guidebook and the facts on the ground, sent by
email to updates@cicerone.co.uk or by post to Cicerone, Juniper House,
Murley Moss, Oxenholme Road, Kendal, LA9 7RL.

**Register your book:** To sign up to receive free updates, special offers
and GPX files where available, register your book in your Cicerone library
at www.cicerone.co.uk.

Front cover: Wonderful reflections of Mont Blanc at the small lake above the Lac
de Brévent (Family Walks, Route 5)

# CONTENTS

### Acknowledgements

Various people have helped with information and without them the whole process would have been a lot more complicated.

I especially want to thank Roger and Mu Portch for their suggestions on good walks with dogs – based on many years of great walks with Bilbo, Sam, Frodo and Pippin. Thanks to Jim Kerr and Caroline Ogden for info and photo. Thanks also to Pete Marland and Pete Blythe who provided photos of their adventures with Roger. Patricia Loffi is my mountain bike consultant and checked several routes as well as suggesting others. Marc Volorio advised on mountain biking, and bouldering, providing some great photos of both. Fred Ancey also let me use some of his spectacular mountain shots and Roger Bassett his charming drawings in Appendix D. Lots of people have walked and climbed with me and hence feature in my photos. There are also a certain number of anonymous models who just happened to be there. I'm grateful to you all.

Finally a huge thankyou to my husband Jon de Montjoye without whom the book would have no maps and a lot more mistakes.

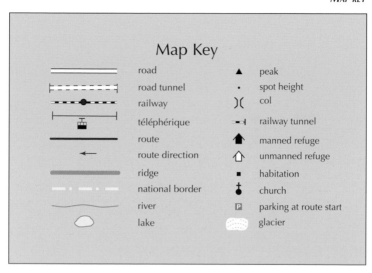

# Map Key

| | | | |
|---|---|---|---|
| ════════ | road | ▲ | peak |
| ┣┅┅┅┅┅┫ | road tunnel | • | spot height |
| ━━●━━━ | railway | )( | col |
| ⬱ | téléphérique | ⊶⊶ | railway tunnel |
| ━━━━━━━ | route | ⬆ | manned refuge |
| ⟵ | route direction | ⬆ | unmanned refuge |
| ━━━━━━━ | ridge | ■ | habitation |
| ─ ▪ ─ ▪ ─ | national border | ✝ | church |
| ‿‿‿‿‿ | river | P | parking at route start |
| ◯ | lake | ▨ | glacier |

## Warning

Mountain walking can be a dangerous activity carrying a risk of personal injury or death. It should be undertaken only by those with a full understanding of the risks and with the training and experience to evaluate them. While every care and effort has been taken in the preparation of this guide, the user should be aware that conditions can be highly variable and can change quickly, materially affecting the seriousness of a mountain walk. Therefore, except for any liability which cannot be excluded by law, neither Cicerone nor the author accept liability for damage of any nature (including damage to property, personal injury or death) arising directly or indirectly from the information in this book.

To call out the Mountain Rescue, use the international emergency number 112: this will connect you via any available network. Once connected to the emergency operator, ask for the police.

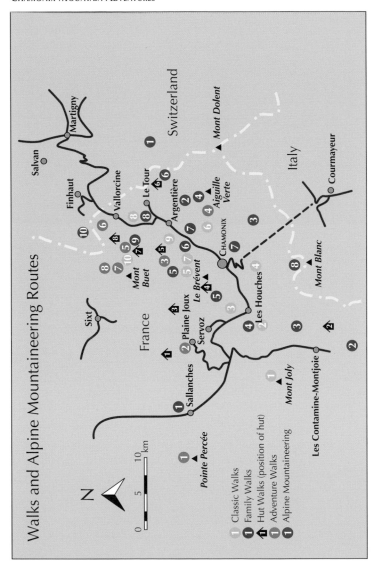

# Walks and Alpine Mountaineering Routes

Classic Walks
Family Walks
Hut Walks (position of hut)
Adventure Walks
Alpine Mountaineering

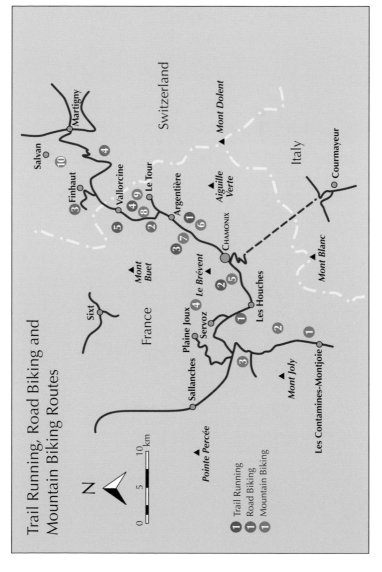

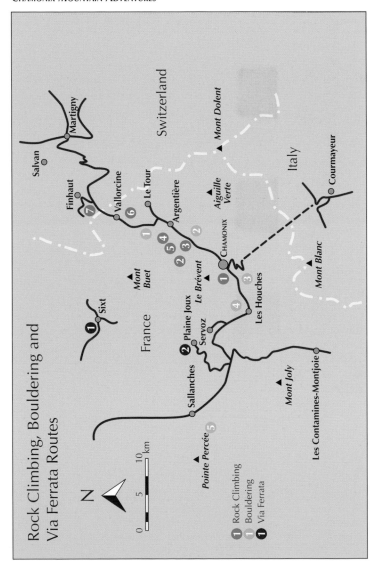

Rock Climbing, Bouldering and Via Ferrata Routes

*At the Col Cornu enjoying splendid views of Mont Blanc (Classic Walk, Route 5)*

*The crux scramble of the Aiguille du Belvédère (Adventure Walks, Route 3)*

# INTRODUCTION

Chamonix, the place of dreams, the home of huge glaciated mountains, including western Europe's highest peak, Mont Blanc; the playground of serious mountaineers...in summer alpinists frequent the sheer rocky faces and steep icy couloirs, in winter extreme skiers launch themselves down audacious slopes and aspirant North Face climbers tackle the cold dark ice faces.

There is another Chamonix, one that offers a plethora of different mountain activities for those who are searching for a mountain holiday not confined to one sport. There are walks both on and off glaciers for all levels; easily accessed climbs for beginners as well as experts; bike rides both on and off road for those just learning how to pedal as well as those looking for daredevil jumps and long hard ascents; miles of trails perfect for runners; and, if you know where to look, there are some very adventurous walks and via ferrata which venture onto terrain normally off limits for non-climbers. Add to this a practical and reliable infrastructure of public transport and lift systems, which make

*The Chamonix Valley seen from the Cosmiques Arête (Alpine Mountaineering, Route 1)*

Chamonix an easily accessible and user-friendly resort. Put succinctly, Chamonix is a playground for anyone looking for adventure in whatever form, against one of the most splendid and inspiring mountain backdrops you could dream of.

This guide aims to open up this world of multi-activity to anyone who wants to explore it. Classic hikes and challenging adventurous expeditions are described, along with walks that will suit all the family, from dog to granny. Regular valley mountain bike routes are included here as well as the very latest in dedicated descents using cable cars and the fabulously spectacular 'Dirt Zones' and bike parks – strictly for those under 30 with shock-absorbing bodies as well as bikes. The most popular and accessible rock-climbing venues are also briefly outlined, with some of the favourite moderate routes described as well as the increasingly popular bouldering sites.

Walks up to mountain huts will appeal to those who fancy a night far from the madness of town, where you can watch the sun set while enjoying true mountain hospitality. Meanwhile, those who like their adventure sprinkled with a frisson of verticality will savour the two via ferratas that are not too far from Chamonix to be feasible in a day.

Finally, other activities are noted and there is a full list of guidebooks for each activity where these exist, in addition to information on resources and valley facilities.

*Approaching the Chéserys Slabs (Rock Climbing, Area 4)*

*Sunset on the Chamonix Aiguilles*

This is a book designed to inspire, to motivate and to inform but it doesn't stand alone: for the walks you'll require a proper map; for climbing, via ferrata and for glacier travel you'll need appropriate experience and equipment, topos and maybe even a Mountain Guide.

This is your starting point – the rest of your adventure is up to you!

## THE REGION

Chamonix is in the Haute Savoie region of France and is situated about an hour's drive from Geneva airport. The valley runs south-west to north-east, with the Vallorcine valley continuing to the Swiss frontier. However, although known as 'Chamonix Mont Blanc', the actual summit of that mountain falls squarely within the territory of Saint-Gervais-les-Bains, which is a source of contention

between the two towns and means that Saint-Gervais can claim the distinction of being the highest municipality in western Europe.

Chamonix is at an altitude of 1050m and the valley in which it lies is formed by the Mont Blanc massif to the east and the Aiguilles Rouges to the west. Originally gouged out by the huge forces of the glaciers, the continuing slow erosion of the valley is now just due to the Arve, the main river.

The Mont Blanc massif itself straddles the frontiers of France, Italy and Switzerland, and travel from Chamonix into Italy and Switzerland is very easy. It is said that Chamonix is the third most visited natural site in the world and certainly on a busy day in high season you could easily believe that all the world is strolling down Chamonix main street!

It's important to get a fix on the two sides of the valley as they provide very different terrain for mountain adventures. Generally, people refer to the north-facing (Mont Blanc massif) and south-facing (Aiguilles Rouges) sides of the valley, although really they are more north-west and south-east facing. The important thing is that the glaciers have to all intents and purposes died away on the north side (Aiguilles Rouges) so this is where you can hike, bike and climb in non-glaciated terrain, while the south side forms the slopes of the massif and that's where you go for snow and ice.

## GLACIERS

Chamonix is dominated by its glaciers and glaciated peaks and they will form the backdrop for almost any hike, ride or climb in the region. The valleys have been carved by ice and what remains of these huge frozen rivers is what many people now come to see.

Chamonix has about 40 glaciers – it's said that from La Flégère cable car top station you can see 14 of them all at once. There are two very striking ones, the Bossons Glacier and the Mer de Glace Glacier. These are each quite different, the Bossons Glacier being very steep and moving at around 250m a year, while the Mer de Glace is relatively flat for much of its length and moves at a leisurely 50m a year. But what they and all other glaciers in the region have in common is that they are very much smaller and shorter than they were 150 years ago.

*The Mer de Glace is certainly shrinking fast but the scenery is nonetheless fabulous (Adventure Walks Route 4)*

Previously the glaciers snaked all the way down to the main Chamonix valley, and 15,000 years ago ice filled the Chamonix valley and onwards all the way to Lyon. The glaciers have been retreating, with small exceptions, for the last 150 years. While this is not the first time that the temperatures have warmed up, it's certainly the fastest change known about and threatens to have consequences far more wide-ranging than just shortening the ski season.

Nevertheless, the glaciated scenery still adds immensely to any mountain adventures in the Chamonix region. The glaciers look their best after a light dusting of snow, giving them a fresh coat of paint. On sunny days the ice picks up the rays and throws them back, glinting and sparkling; on cloudy days the glaciers reflect the grey. So pick your activities carefully – save those especially picturesque hikes, climbs and rides for a perfect day.

*Alpenrose*

## FLOWERS AND ANIMALS

Whether you're hiking, climbing, running or biking, there's lots to see in the Alps. Throughout the summer there will be flowers to spot, from abundant valley flowers in the meadows early in the season, to tiny alpine rarities at high altitude as the season progresses.

Some easy ones to identify are:

- **Alpenrose** A rhododendron bush present from the valley floor up to about 2500m. The pink alpenrose flowers carpet the slopes throughout July.
- **Trumpet gentians** These are the first gentians to appear and are bright blue and trumpet shaped.
- **Alpine gentians** Tiny blue stars above about 2000m.
- **Edelweiss** Usually found on limestone terrain so they are few and far between in the Chamonix valley but could well be spotted in the limestone foothills, and in people's gardens.
- **Houseleek** Commonly grows on rocks or house roofs. This succulent plant can grow in very little earth and is to be found low down in the valleys in early summer, where it grows quite tall

Martagon Lily

(around 30cm is not unusual). A different variant is also found way up, on the highest slopes, around 2500–3000m and is tiny with striking deep pink flowers.

- **Martagon lily** You might spot one of these exotic pink flowers during July, usually around 1200–1800m, often among vegetation. They are protected and very special.

The forest is also interesting. The main trees in the Chamonix forests are:

- **Larch** Providing the best wood for building, this tree has enough resin in its trunk to not need any treatment when used for construction. All the old reddish-coloured wooden chalets in the valley are made from larch. It's also used for

Larch

ship's masts as it grows tall and straight. This deciduous conifer loses its needles in winter, which means it turns a nice golden tinge in the autumn giving some colour to the slopes.

- **Spruce** These are the classic Christmas trees, green all year round. Most Chamonix forest largely consists of larch and spruce.

- **Silver birch** These light grey trees are common at valley level. They are often bent over from the winter snow but are generally supple enough to bear it.

- **Arolla pine** Often seen at the upper edge of the treeline, these long needled pines have very heavy seeds, much favoured by birds, which tend to store them in rocky crevices where the seeds then set roots. Very slow to grow, these sturdy trees can reach several hundred years old.

- **Alder** More of a bush than a tree, the alder is often found on forested hillsides, where there are gullies bare of any other trees. These are slopes that avalanche routinely in the winter and the alder is the only tree that likes such wet and mobile conditions.

There are also lots of wild animals and birds inhabiting the valley and slopes. A quiet approach is more likely to give you a sighting, but sometimes the animal will either be unaware of your presence or just not care. During your stay you'll probably catch at least

Marmot

fleeting glimpses of alpine animals. Here's the list of the main ones to watch out for.

- **Marmots** Usually heard rather than seen at first as their high-pitched warning whistle gives away their presence. Keep your eyes open on rocky slopes or grassy meadows.

- **Chamois** Often spotted early morning or late evening in the higher forests. This goat–deer hybrid has small horns that hook backwards and long legs.

- **Ibex** This mountain goat prefers rocky terrain and will be found high up on shaly rocky slopes. It's a sturdy creature, often seen in groups, but if you're lucky enough to come across an old male he'll most likely be alone.

21

Ibex are seen quite often but not always this close

- **Stoats** These energetic little creatures will sometimes be spotted scurrying around boulders. They look sweet but can be vicious to anyone outside of family. In winter they are white with a black tip to their tails and called ermine.

- **Deer** Small deer (*chevreuil*) are quite commonly seen in the forests, usually from behind as they make a fast getaway. Larger deer are less commonly spotted although at night they often cross the roads and care should be taken when driving around the Chamonix valley after dark. Whether you see them or not, the deer are there in the forest and their droppings are often seen.

You're most likely to encounter them at dusk.

- **Foxes** These are numerous in the Chamonix region but luckily haven't yet adopted the habits of the town fox, which is seen as a pest. Foxes here live wild and so far don't seem to be too interested in the McDustbin ready meal... long may it stay like this.

- **Vipers** These snakes are commonly found on hot tracks in the afternoon – there's a fair chance of coming across one slumbering on the trail if you're at reasonably low altitude (below 1000m). Getting bitten hurts and you'll need medical attention, so be careful where you put your feet and don't wear sandals when hiking.

*Apollo butterfly*

- **Butterflies** On southern slopes expect to see lots of butterflies in the height of the summer. The large white Apollo is easy to spot as it flits around slowly from flower to flower.
- **Golden eagle** If you look up and see a big bird circling over Vallorcine or Chamonix, the chances are it's a golden eagle. They have a huge wingspan – well over 2m – and so they don't need to flap much. The immature adults have white marks on the underside of their wings, which makes for easier identification.
- **Alpine chough** These black birds have a yellow beak and red feet and they will almost certainly join you at some point in the mountains for a picnic. They make a characteristic cheeping sound and are usually found at frequented passes and huts.
- **Bearded vulture** There are a few of these around, since they have been reintroduced in the Aravis range, just down the valley. These wonderful birds have a wing-span of almost 3m and an orange underbelly. If you see one, count yourself lucky. And don't panic – they only eat bones.

There are lots more flowers, trees and animals to look out for, of course – this is just a very small selection. Basic flora and fauna books are available in English from the bookstores in Chamonix. Armed with these you'll add another dimension to your walks, climbs and bike rides.

## HOW IT ALL STARTED

The history of Chamonix is first documented in 1091, when an order of monks settled on the right bank of the Arve and the Priory was formed. No doubt people inhabited the valley for centuries before this; but living tucked away among the high mountains, cut off from the lower valleys for a good six months of the year and the rest of the time struggling to scrape some sort of existence, the inhabitants of the Chamonix valley didn't attract any attention for many centuries.

Traditionally the peaks and glaciers struck fear into the hearts of the locals; the source of violent storms, avalanches, mud slides, often wreathed

*The first ascensionists of Mont Blanc*

in clouds and battered by winds, such places could only be the cursed home of dragons and evil spirits.

The glaciers themselves gave cause for great concern in the 18th century when what is now referred to as the 'Little Ice Age' occurred. This caused the glaciers to increase in size at an alarming rate, pushing these frozen rivers down into the valleys where they threatened to destroy homes and farmland.

However, not everyone shared this fear of the glaciers and the destiny of Chamonix changed in 1741 when two English chaps, Wyndham and Pococke, set off from Geneva to visit Chamonix and discovered this rural mountain village, where people struggled to survive on what they could

cultivate during the short summer season. Wyndham and Pococke were mesmerised and enchanted by the glaciers and having visited the Mer de Glace they left and spread the word. Soon, well-heeled visitors were flocking to Chamonix from all over Europe and it became a sought-after feature on any European Tour. By the 1770s, it is estimated that 1500 people a year were visiting Chamonix. The locals were quick to seize the opportunity and soon teams of 'guides' and porters were ready to lead these tourists onto the glaciers. Summit ascents soon followed, with Mont Blanc itself first climbed in 1786.

This growth in tourism equally lead to the construction of hotels and the formation of the Compagnie des

*The Mer de Glace seen from the air*

Guides de Chamonix in the early 19th century. In 1860 a road was built from Geneva to Chamonix, via Sallanches. This was also the year that Chamonix became French, having previously been attached to the mountain Kingdom of Savoy.

In 1901 the railway arrived in Chamonix, which enabled travel in winter, and by the middle of the 20th century not only did Chamonix boast a mountain railway and numerous cable cars but the town had also hosted the first Winter Olympics in 1924.

Today, Chamonix sees its permanent population grow from around 10,000 to 60,000 in the summer season, and on a sunny summer's day more than 200 people may stand on the summit of Mont Blanc.

## MOUNTAIN ADVENTURES

The valley base itself provides the full range of activities at a lower level. Whatever activity you decide on, it will be done against a jaw-dropping backdrop of glaciated peaks, soaring rocky spires, and deep rivers and gorges.

### Walks

First and foremost, Chamonix is a region where people walk in the hills and it makes sense that this guide features lots of walks. Any walk can be an adventure, a discovery of a new path, a surprising view, a summit or a hamlet. One person's stroll is another person's challenge, so the walks are divided into different categories:

*The beautiful Tré-les-Eaux valley (Adventure Walks, Route 5)*

**Classic Walks**

These are the walks people come to Chamonix to do, the real classics, although obviously the choice is somewhat subjective. They vary in length but they almost all require hiking fitness and, apart from one hike, they involve significant ascent.

**Family Walks**

These are walks that can be done by most people, committed hikers or not. Children, dogs, the elderly – everyone can come along. However, check the details for each walk – there are some places where dogs have to be kept on a lead or not even taken at all. These walks all take you to scenic vistas and on pleasant trails, but without the relentless climbs so often a

feature of alpine ascents, and without any dodgy bits for those who are not steady on their feet or who are totally unaware of danger.

**Hut Walks**

A hut provides a marvellous objective for a walk, maybe just for lunch or to spend the night. Huts are always interesting and are often an opportunity to meet local people and sample some regional specialities. Most huts enjoy fine views and a night spent in a mountain hut will almost always be an unforgettable experience – for various reasons. Even if you're not keen on sleeping in close proximity to lots of other people, the evening spent watching the sunset from the terrace while sipping a home-made *digestif* and the morning with breakfast taken in the early sunshine while the rest of Chamonix is still in deep shade, should make it all worthwhile. If in doubt, just go for lunch.

**Adventure Walks**

These are the hikes that require lots of energy and a steady footing, and often a desire for an exposed ridge, a scramble or just a really challenging day out. These are not for children or dogs, and the times and distances should be taken into account.

**Alpine mountaineering**

While this book does not aim to describe hard climbs and ascents in

## THE EMOSSON LAKES REGION

The Lac d'Emosson and the Lac du Vieux Emosson are located to the north of Chamonix, just over the border in Switzerland. They form the northern edge of the area covered in this guide, and several walks are described there.

*Emosson Lake*

The dam itself is a huge sweeping structure, which has an amazing climbing route on artificial holds. Just watching climbers on this is likely to leave you with sweating hands and a racing heart but if you're up for it then details are to be had at the restaurant. Access is strictly controlled; you can't just go and do it! Equally spectacular is the tyrolien (Pures Emossons) which provides a guaranteed adrenaline rush. Again, sign up at the restaurant.

But the lake is also (somewhat paradoxically) an area of great tranquility and beauty. As soon as you leave the busy parking and dam area you'll find yourself in beautiful scenery with a wealth of trails to choose from to take you along the lakeside or into the high surrounding peaks.

There is an attractive transport option (Vertic'alp Emosson) to reach the Emosson Lake: a funicular, tram and mini funicular which go from Châtelard frontier station. This is closed for the 2022 season. Check for updates www.verticalp-emosson.ch/en.

*Abseiling on the Cosmiques Arête (Alpine Mountaineering, Route 7)*

the high mountains, there are glacier hikes and climbs that can be seen as entry-level routes to take hill-walkers onto glaciers, up to summits and onto rocky scrambles, but at a reasonably accessible standard.

Venturing onto the glaciers was once considered suicidal, which is why it took so long for anyone to find a route up Mont Blanc. These days, glacier travel is pretty routine for many mountaineers, but the attendant dangers haven't really changed, except that it has been established that dragons probably don't inhabit the peaks, or if they do they're fairly innocuous.

The routes in this guide can be planned for a first alpine season, but it must be stressed that mountaineering in the Alps is potentially a deadly activity and each alpine summer sees many accidents on the peaks and glaciers, some of them fatal. Appropriate knowledge and training must be undertaken to climb safely in the high mountains and for this reason these walks and climbs are very often done with professional guides.

## Mountain biking

Chamonix has embraced the evolution of mountain biking over the last 20 years or so and now has several dedicated venues for descent and aerobatics. These places are briefly described in this book, but there are also lots of trails that lend themselves to knobbly tyres and low gears and the best of these rides are described.

*Mountain biking near Le Tour (photo: Marc Volorio)*

However, the relationship between hikers and bikers remains fragile, so restrictions have been set and some trails are off limits, especially in the peak holiday season, July and August. Nevertheless, bikers and hikers can live in harmony and, thanks to these clear regulations, there are some really good rides where any mountain biker, from beginner to expert, can have a great time and not be shouted at or risk killing anyone in the process. A series of rides are detailed in this book, and reference is made to other resources for those who decide riding the trails is for them.

### Road biking

Cycling on the road in the Alps has its roots in deep-seated tradition, with the annual Tour de France always passing through the alpine chain within view of Mont Blanc. However, until fairly recently it seemed to be the preserve of the bronzed and honed Lance Armstrong look-alikes. The last few years have seen an explosion in the popularity of the sport and now, as soon as the roads are snow-free,

cyclists of all abilities are to be seen powering and puffing their way up the local passes. And there's certainly plenty to go at, from the major passes of the Haute Savoie to minor roads that give a more varied and less relentless ride. There are also options to make life easier by riding from one place to another and taking the train back.

### Trail running

Trail running is another activity that has massively increased in popularity in the last few years. Time was, when the odd lightly clad runner smoking past overburdened hikers on the trail was a fairly rare occurrence. Now it's quite normal, especially when one of the local races is coming up. These days, people run year round in Chamonix, taking to the hard-packed snowy valley trails in the depth of winter. The prestigious Ultra Trail du Mont Blanc has ensured that Chamonix is fast becoming the Holy Grail of mountain running – and with good cause, given the vast array of trails available.

**Rock climbing and bouldering**

Chamonix has a whole collection of crags in the valley, with approaches of just a few minutes. These crags all offer bolted climbing, with lots of routes in the more moderate grade range. Many crags are suitable for children too (as long as they're well-behaved!). Just a few routes on each of the selected crags are described, but if sampling these climbs makes you want more, the local guidebooks will ensure a lifetime of climbing adventures.

In addition to the roped brigade, more and more climbers seem to have decided to forego the time, expense and weight of ropes and gear, and have taken to walking around with big pads. Several bouldering sites in and around the Chamonix valley cater to the needs of the Pad People.

**Via ferratas**

It's perhaps surprising, but there are no real via ferratas in the Chamonix and Vallorcine valleys. There are lots of cabled sections of path (which often feature on the Adventure Walks) and some mountain hut approaches are enabled by ladders and chains. But there are no via ferratas where you need to use proper gear and where the cabled way is purely an entity in itself. However, if this is what you want to do, do not despair. An hour or so's drive from Chamonix gives access to several via ferratas in

*Sunny climbing on perfect rock at the central sector of Les Chéserys*

the Haute Savoie region, all of which are listed here and two of which are described.

## OTHER ACTIVITIES

There are lots of other sporty activities to occupy you in and around Chamonix. Here are some of them:

- **Golf** Chamonix boasts a fine course, the big attraction being the backdrop of prestigious peaks – Mont Blanc, the Drus, the Aiguille Verte, the Chamonix Needles … it doesn't come much more scenic than this! Open every day from late April to early November.
- **Tennis** The courts are just off the Place Mont Blanc near the river and are open from early May to the end of September.
- **Swimming** The swimming centre has had a recent makeover and features various pools, indoors and out, with lots of exciting slides and other aquatic joys. Also near the Place Mont Blanc.
- **Skating rink** There's an indoor Olympic rink and outdoor rink in winter, next to the swimming pool.
- **Paragliding** Known as *parapente* in French, there are several take-off points from the Chamonix lifts. There is a special lift pass for paragliders. There are also several companies offering tandem rides. The world championships are regularly held at the Planpraz lift

*Planpraz is one of the main take-off zones for paragliders*

and this is a good place to go any hot summer's day to watch people taking off. During July and August take-off is forbidden from the Aiguille du Midi.
- **Rafting** The River Arve seems to give a great rafting experience and there are several companies offering this in Chamonix.
- **Canyoning** Various good canyoning sites exist in and around Chamonix. The Compagnie de Guides in Chamonix offer guided descents.
- **Summer luge** This thrilling toboggan ride is accessed by a chairlift at Les Planards, near the centre of town, just after the road crossing of the Montenvers railway.

*Canyoning at Barberine, near Vallorcine*

- **Indoor climbing** There is a climbing wall at Les Houches for you to hone your skills.

**Rainy day activities**

Just occasionally it rains in Chamonix. Of course, hiking and biking are perfectly feasible in the rain but once the attraction of this wears off you might be looking for drier activities.

- The cinema often has films in English.
- The Alpine Museum is a good way to while away an afternoon.
- The Espace Tairraz has a fascinating crystals museum, the Musée des Cristaux. There is also an interactive alpine exhibition. An entrance ticket here also gets you entry to the Alpine Museum.
- The Petit Train Touristique offers a tour of town with guided commentary and would more or less keep you dry in the rain.

- The train journey to Martigny is worth doing and, once there, the St Bernard Dogs Museum is fun if you like dogs. The museum also contains an excellent historical overview of the region. The Fondation Pierre Gianadda exhibition centre, just across the road from the museum, is renowned among art lovers.
- The thermal baths in Saint-Gervais-les-Bains (www.thermes-saint-gervais.com) are not far away. Offering all sorts of cures and treatments, they provide a very relaxing way to spend a day during a mountain holiday.

And, finally, if it's pouring with rain on the French side of Mont Blanc, it's just possible it will be sunny on the Italian side. A bus service runs from Chamonix to Courmayeur, through the Mont Blanc Tunnel.

## WHEN TO GO

This partly depends on the activities you're intending to do, but everything in this guide requires at least semi-summer conditions – in other words, the winter snow should have melted off most slopes. July and August are high season in Chamonix and at that time everything is open – hotels, cafés, huts and lifts. The latter are important for some walks and for certain types of mountain biking. However, June and September are also lovely months in the Alps, but be aware that if you're depending on

*Excitement guaranteed on the huge tyrolien descent at Emosson*

lifts or want to have the full choice of life in town, then this is not the time to come. On the other hand, for those who like peace and quiet the busy season from mid-July to mid-August is probably to be avoided.

As for the weather, this can be anything, anytime. The mountains create their own weather system so it's impossible to say that one month will be better than another. There are a few pointers, though:

• If the weather becomes hot, it's likely that storms will build up during the day. In this case it's important to get going early in the morning so as to be finished before any storm activity. This is especially important if you're going into the high mountains, on ridges, or on via ferratas or any cabled way.

• Bad weather, if it comes, usually doesn't last very long. It's far more likely to be really bad for a day or so then clear up than to be moderately rainy for a whole week.

• Rain in the valley is more than likely to fall as snow above 3000m or sometimes lower.

• If it's pouring with rain in Chamonix, it might well be bright and sunny on the Italian side of the massif, in Courmayeur.

• Finally, these are the Alps – they are snowy at the top and green lower down. There is a reason for this beauty: it rains sometimes. Otherwise it would be desert.

33

## GETTING THERE AND GETTING AROUND

Chamonix is only an hour from Geneva airport, which is served by many airlines including some 'low-cost' ones. Various companies offer competitively priced transfers from the airport to Chamonix itself, but beware, some may require a full bus to guarantee the price.

Arrival by train is fairly simple. The Eurostar runs from the UK to Paris, where the TGV service will beam you to Saint-Gervais–Le Fayet in just a few hours. From there the train to Chamonix runs hourly.

Chamonix is well served by public transport. The Mont Blanc Express train runs from Saint-Gervais–Le Fayet to Martigny every hour. This train can take bikes – five bikes per train is the official limit. The Chamonix Bus runs up and down the valley, as far as the Col des Montets in the summer. There is also a dedicated Chamonix Bus for bikes, with four services a day between Chamonix–Col des Montets and Chamonix–Le Tour.

If you're using Chamonix accommodation then you can get a *Carte d'Hôte* card on arrival. This allows free travel on the train between Servoz and Vallorcine and on the Chamonix Bus.

## ACCOMMODATION

There is a host of possibilities in and around Chamonix of all standards, from hotels (ranging from basic to luxurious) to *gîtes* to self-catering apartments to huts to campsites. But beware, many hotels are closed after the winter until mid-June, and during

*The Mont Blanc Express makes it easy to get about*

*The Cabane du Trient (photo: Nigel Jones)*

the French holidays (July and August) many hotels will be full, especially during the period 14 July–15 August. Reservation in advance at whatever type accommodation during this time is highly recommended.

### Hotels

These range from five-star luxury to no-star basic. Chamonix itself has many hotels covering the full range, while the smaller places in the valley generally offer a more limited choice. Chamonix Tourist Office (www.chamonix.com) offers a reservation service and will also search for rooms available for a particular date.

### Gîtes

There are two types of gîte: a regular gîte is a house available for rent for self-catering accommodation – these will often be big enough for several families; the other version is the gîte d'étape which offers basic accommodation in rooms or dormitories, with dinner and breakfast. These can be very good value and an excellent way to sample local food and culture.

### Campsites

There are several sites in Chamonix itself and along the valley. Camping is generally not allowed outside of campsites.

### Huts or refuges

It can be very pleasant to spend a night or two in a mountain hut when exploring the area. These vary greatly in the facilities they offer, from quite

35

luxurious with showers and rooms to the most basic with just a dormitory and dining room. There are always toilets in or near the huts and usually in summer there is running cold water, but in high huts this can freeze overnight, meaning there is no water in the morning. Water in the huts is not always potable so you may need to buy bottled water.

Most huts are open from mid to late June to mid-September and there will be a guardian in residence. The guardian will cook the evening meal and breakfast, and many huts also offer picnic lunches too. They serve drinks, both soft and alcoholic. In some huts you can prepare your own food but this isn't common in the huts described in this guide.

All huts described here have bedding and usually hut slippers are available, although this is not always the case.

**Hut etiquette**
You should always reserve at a hut before going, even if it's just a phone call the night before. And it goes without saying that if you can't get there for some reason you should call to cancel. If you have special dietary requirements then you should tell the guardian when you make your reservation. Equally, if you prefer to be in a room (if they exist) you should ask for that beforehand. There are no single-sex dormitories in European huts.

You should also ask about payment – some huts take credit cards but more often than not you pay in cash.

On arrival at a hut for the night you should greet the guardian and tell them who you are. At most huts you're expected to remove your boots before going into the living area. The hut guardian will tell you what the procedures are for things like eating and rooms. Each hut is different, but the common factor is that the hut is the guardian's home for the season and so you should treat the hut like someone else's house.

On the Office de la Haute Montagne/La Chamoniarde website (www.chamoniarde.com) you can find a list of all huts in the Mont Blanc massif with the dates they are open as well as contact numbers (see also Appendix A).

---

### TOURIST INFORMATION

The Chamonix valley is served by several tourist offices, the main one of which, in Chamonix itself, has information for the whole valley. If you are looking for information about the smaller villages, you can go straight to their respective tourist offices. (See Appendix A for contact information.)

Much information can be gleaned from the Office de Haute Montagne (OHM), also known as La Chamoniarde www.chamoniarde. com, tel 04 50 53 22 08) in Chamonix and this is definitely a place to get to know. Situated next to the church, in the same building as the Compagnie des Guides de Chamonix, the OHM is

*Starting up the chains in the Tré-les-Eaux valley (Adventure Walks, Route 5)*

open to all. Guidebooks and maps are available for consultation, and there is always someone on hand who will be able to update you on current conditions in the mountains. The weather forecast is also displayed in French and English on the wall outside.

## LANGUAGE

The language officially spoken in Chamonix is, of course, French. Chamonix itself is now so international that English (or a version thereof) is heard almost as much as French. However, having a smattering of French vocabulary is advisable and will endear you to the locals. At least greet people with '*Bonjour*' and offer an '*Au revoir*' when you leave. Add in a '*Bonne journée*' and you'll be doing well. '*S'il vous plaît*' and '*Merci*' tend to get you a smile too.

It is normal practice in France to say a greeting even in shops and Anglophones can appear quite rude if they don't follow this custom. In the mountains '*Bonjour*' is also expected, whether on foot, on a bike or at a belay on a climb.

A list of useful words and phrases is included in the glossary (Appendix B).

## HEALTH AND SAFETY

There are risks attached to all mountain activities, however safe the environment may seem. Accidents in the non-glaciated mountains range from sprained ankles to broken bones to much worse – some of the delightful

37

trails described here traverse mountain sides where a fall off the path would probably have terrible consequences. Equally, mountain biking can be dangerous if you're on a narrow trail or doing a fast descent. The glaciated hikes have their own associated risks, as do rock climbing and via ferratas.

Having taken all sensible precautions then these activities are there to be enjoyed, but it is crucial to do what you can to avoid accidents and then be prepared if they do happen.

**Weather forecasts**

Before you go out, it's important to check the weather forecast. For an up-to-date weather forecast in French, go to: http://france.meteofrance.com. The following websites also have forecasts in English: www.chamonix-meteo.com and www.chamonix.com.

**First aid**

All walkers and climbers should carry a small basic first aid kit in their rucksacks. This should contain:

- Plasters
- Painkillers
- Antiseptic cream
- Crêpe bandage
- Penknife with scissors
- Latex gloves
- Antiseptic wipes

*At the top of the Cosmiques Arête (Alpine Mountaineering, Route 3)*

**Help required**
Raise both arms above head to form a 'Y'

**Help not required**
Raise one arm above head and extend the other downward, to form the diagonal of an 'N'

## Emergencies

As a last resort for serious injuries you may need to contact the emergency services. The number to call is 112. This works throughout Europe.

In Chamonix the rescue service is run by the PGHM and they can be contacted directly on tel 04 50 53 16 89. It is also possible to send an SMS, which can be helpful if your mobile battery is low or the reception is very poor. You need to be able to tell them:

- Where – your exact location
- What – the precise nature of the problem
- Who – how many people and in what condition
- When – exactly when the accident happened

## Rescue

Any rescue in the Alps is likely to be carried out by helicopter. Make your position visible for the helicopter and keep everyone and everything together, out of the way.

When the helicopter approaches, signal that you are the person who called by raising both arms diagonally. This tells the pilot, 'Yes, I need help' and 'Yes, land here'.

If you do not need help raise one arm up diagonally and one arm down diagonally. This tells the pilot, 'No, I do not need help' or 'No, do not land here'.

## Insurance

Rescue and medical costs are charged in Europe so you do need insurance. The following companies provide good insurance schemes:

- The British Mountaineering Council www.thebmc.co.uk
- Snowcard www.snowcard.co.uk
- Global Rescue www.globalrescue.com
- Austrian Alpine Club www.aacuk.org.uk
- Club Alpin Français www.ffcam.fr

## How to hire a mountain guide

As mentioned, all the activities in this guide have associated guides or instructors and hiring such a person to take you on your chosen route, whatever it may be, should enhance your experience in many ways, while reducing or eliminating some of the potential for either failing on the route for one reason or another or having rather more of an 'adventure' than expected or desired.

Sometimes taking a guide is not just to provide a better day or a longer route; it's actually a question of safety and in some situations may save you from disaster. The mountaineering routes in this book are inherently dangerous, so if you want to hike on the glaciers or climb the high peaks you either need to know what you're doing or take along someone who does.

Chamonix has several guiding companies, the most well known and established being the town's own group of guides, the Compagnie des Guides (www.chamonix-guides.com), which works out of the same building as the Office de Haute Montagne next to the church. Alternatively there are lots of independent guides of all nationalities, including the author's own company Trekking in the Alps (www.trekkinginthealps.com), some of whom are resident full-time in Chamonix while others just spend the season in the area.

If you decide to hire a guide, it's best to contact the company or person in advance and find out whether they are willing to guide your chosen route, what prior training they require of you, how many days they expect you to hire them for and what is their policy in case of bad weather.

Some routes, such as the glacier hikes, can usually be done without training days with the guide, whereas for Mont Blanc the guide will usually

require that you do some acclimatisation routes beforehand, usually guided. It should be noted that Mont Blanc is subject to certain norms of guiding: a guide can take only one or two clients at a time and there is an established tariff.

When hiring a guide you should ask for their credentials. Here are the certifications required to guide in France:

- **Hiking on non-glaciated terrain** Accompagnateur en Montagne/ International Mountain Leader; Guide de Haute Montagne/ High Mountain Guide (IFMGA certified)
- **Hiking and climbing on glaciers** Guide de Haute Montagne/ High Mountain Guide (IFMGA certified)
- **Via ferrata** Moniteur d'escalade; Guide de Haute Montagne/ High Mountain Guide (IFMGA certified)
- **Rock climbing** Moniteur d'escalade; Guide de Haute Montagne/High Mountain Guide (IFMGA certified)
- **Mountain biking** Accompagnateur en Montagne with VTT qualification; Moniteur de VTT
- **Road biking** Moniteur Cycliste

## USING THIS GUIDE

This is intended to be a guide to introduce you to lots of different activities, sending you in the right direction, giving you the basics but not a

Nearing the end of the Crochues traverse
(Alpine Mountaineering, Route 5)

comprehensive guide to each activity. It is weighted towards hill walking at many different levels, but there is also plenty of information regarding travel on two wheels and for those who want to scale the cliffs of the region by whatever means. Local guidebooks for each activity are mentioned, where available.

If you're coming to Chamonix with your family or a group of friends with different interests, or if yourself fancy branching out and trying lots of adventures in the mountains rather than concentrating on one, then this is the book to buy.

**Grades and timings**

The walks are graded as Alpine Mountaineering, Adventure, Classic, Hut and Family. No further grades

are given (apart from for Alpine Mountaineering routes); but each walk has distance (except Alpine Mountaineering) and altitude gain and you'll get a good idea of what's involved from the category a walk falls into and from information given in the text.

Timings are given for walks, but these are a guideline only. Do not treat the timings as a challenge. They are generally based on an ascent of 300m per hour or around 4km an hour.

For mountain biking the timings are based on those given in local information. For climbing timings are not appropriate, as the routes in this guide are generally one pitch or very short multi-pitch. The times given for via ferrata come from local information.

Road biking is so variable in speed that timings are not really possible. I know from personal experience that cyclists have very different speeds, not only for ascents but also for descents, so any attempt to give a timing seems to be of no real use. Distances and altitudes are given and this should be enough to calculate whether you'll be back for lunch or should take a picnic.

## Maps

The French Institut Géographique National Top 25 series maps are the best for the activities described here. The ones needed are:

- 3630 OT Chamonix Mont Blanc
- 3531 ET Saint-Gervais-les-Bains
- 3530 ET Samoëns
- 3531 OT Megève
- 3530 OT Cluses Sallanches

A 1:50,000 map is useful to get an overview of the region, and for the road biking routes. The whole area is covered by the IGN Rando Editions map A1 Alpes Pays du Mont Blanc.

If you use a GPS, programme it to datum WGS84 and grid system UTM/UPS otherwise all grid references will be inaccurate.

Referred to as cable cars, chairlifts or gondolas, lifts are written in French as *téléphérique*, *télésiège* and *télécabine* and shown with a symbol on the maps.

## Equipment

While some activities require more gear than others, and the knowledge of how to use it, certain essentials are common to all mountain activities. A map and compass are recommended unless you already know where you're

*A well-equipped hiker is a happy one. Descending from the Grands Montets (Alpine Mountaineering, Route 2)*

*Sometimes you have to wonder why you bothered taking the bike...*

going. Even then, you'll be out in the hills where the weather can change and fog can make it difficult to find your way back, so it would seem prudent to always go equipped with navigation tools. The other gear that is common for all activities is appropriate warm clothing, drink and some food, as well as the first aid kit mentioned above.

Other gear is particular to different activities, as outlined below.

## Walking

First and foremost, whichever walks you go for, this guide alone will not suffice; you need to buy the local 1:25,000 maps. This book includes sketch maps for each route, but these do not stand alone – they are for location and guidance before you set out.

Other requirements are basic, but essentials shouldn't be overlooked – the weather can change very quickly in the Alps and a hail storm at 2500m can have serious consequences if you don't have any warm gear. Shoes or boots should have good soles, as a slip can be fatal even on the simplest alpine path. Trekking poles are optional but make life easier, faster and less arduous.

## Alpine mountaineering

As well as regular walking equipment, glacier travel requires gear – crampons, harness, rope and associated hardware. You need to know how to travel safely on a glacier and these skills can only be learnt in practice. (See Appendix D.) If in doubt take a High Mountain Guide.

43

### Trail running

The trails in Chamonix are often rocky and a slip can have bad consequences. Running shoes with a really good sole are essential. Many people use very lightweight poles for ultra-long runs. A hydration sac is better than a bottle in hot conditions as more fluid can be carried on your back, whereas a hand-held bottle can be cumbersome when running on trails.

### Mountain biking

Again, a map is essential otherwise you can quickly get quite confused if not lost.

Depending on the type of riding you plan to do, the bike needs to have some degree of suspension. You can rent all types of bikes in Chamonix and the shop assistants are experts in their sport. It goes without saying that a helmet is essential and you will probably want some sort of padded body armour for the wild descent rides.

### Road biking

Besides a helmet and a water bottle you will need a windproof jacket – while the ascents can be very hot, those fast descents will soon chill your body. Gloves are also a good idea, both for protection and warmth on the descents.

### Rock climbing and bouldering

Harness, rock boots and chalk bag are the obvious requirements for rock climbing. All the routes described in this guide (except those on the Index) are fully bolted so there's no need for nuts and friends, just a rack of quickdraws. Rope lengths, single or double, are noted for each crag. A helmet is strongly recommended. Bouldering is the simplest of sports (just rock boots and chalk required) but a pad seems *de rigueur* nowadays. A good spotter is also useful.

### Via ferrata

In addition to a harness, it is essential to have a special via ferrata lanyard – a climbing sling is not adequate as a fall onto a regular sling is likely to break your back. A helmet is essential.

### Taking your dog

Many people will come to Chamonix on a low-cost flight and therefore

*Skip, Rifugio du Bonatti 1998–2013*

*My intrepid mountain cat, Zig*

it's likely Doggy will stay at home. However, now that pets can travel in Europe more easily, some people do drive to Chamonix for a long holiday and their furry friends come too.

There are important regulations on where you can take your dog and in the Family Walks descriptions I have noted whether dogs are welcome on the trails.

Dogs are not allowed at all in the following reserves:
• Aiguille Rouges Reserve
• Merlet Reserve
• Platé Reserve
• Carlaveyron Reserve

They are tolerated on a lead in the Bérard Reserve and at Loriaz.

However, you should be aware that if you take your dog and you see cattle or sheep grazing you should keep it on a lead. And if Fido is in tow, you're far less likely to see any wildlife – not only his presence but also his odour will see to that.

On the other hand, you can take your cat anywhere you like.

45

# 1 WALKS

## CLASSIC WALKS

What makes a Classic Walk? It goes without saying that the views should be stunning and if possible in all directions; the terrain should be varied and interesting, hopefully with some forest but also lots of walking above the treeline; a clear objective, such as a summit; and maybe even a cafe en route or at the end for a cold beer or an ice cream while you sit back and soak up the scenery.

There are so many walks in the Chamonix region that it's difficult to choose. Ten of the best – or perhaps the best 10! – are included here.

## FAMILY WALKS

Family Walks are intended to be walks that anyone and everyone can do, including small children, reluctant adolescents and people who don't want to walk very far.

Some are longer than others, but all offer lovely scenery and most are feasible in summertime, regardless of the weather. Routes 2 and 10 are harder than the others and should be reserved for the day when all the family are feeling super fit and the weather is perfect.

For dog lovers, I have noted whether your beloved furry friend

*Mont Blanc as backdrop while walking near the Refuge Bel Lachat (Hut Walks, Route 4)*

*Hiking in the Alps for all the family*

can go along too. Where dogs are not allowed this is usually because the area is a designated reserve of some kind. Sometimes dogs are allowed but must be kept on a lead – usually because of the presence of farm animals.

### HUT WALKS

A hut makes a good objective for a walk, either to stay the night so as to climb to a high point the next day, or as a destination in itself as a good and interesting day out, usually with the added incentive of lunch and a stunning view once you reach your goal. It's usually a bonus if you can stay the night as the evening and morning light, in good weather, give

by far the best photos and ambience. Moreover, many huts are really busy in the day with the lunchtime trade, but when those people leave around mid-afternoon a wonderful calm and tranquillity settle on the high pastures and mountainsides. Of course, if you happen to hit the night when several families with screaming kids stay at the hut, you might regret your over-night reservation!

In and around the Chamonix valley the choice of huts is vast, many of them situated in the non-glaciated *moyenne montagne*, with an approach walk of 1–3hr – perfect for a pre and post-lunch walk, with the added incentive that usually the return will be largely downhill.

Choose your hut carefully and you'll be able to take dog, child and granny, but be careful – several huts described here are in reserves where dogs are not welcome, even on a leash. It's not usually a good idea to take your dog on an overnight stay in a hut – not only might there be a resident hut dog, or indeed hut cat, but also other people staying might not be quite so keen to share with your canine friend.

In the summer season (early July to late August) any hut described here will be open, but outside that time it's worth phoning ahead to check or asking at the Office de la Montagne. It would be rather disappointing to hike all the way up there and arrive gasping for a beer and *tartiflette* to find the little *fermé* sign on the firmly barred door. I have tried to give up-to-date details on facilities at the huts, but bear in mind that sometimes showers might be cold, or temporarily unavailable, rooms might be full, or the hut may have been recently refurbished and what I describe as 'basic' may be transformed into a luxury mountain lodge!

Almost all the hut walks described here are there-and-back routes, the return following the outward route.

## ADVENTURE WALKS

All walks can be adventurous on different levels – it's always exciting to discover a new route, and an unexpected view – but the walks described here also all involve some use of cables or chains along the way. These 'equipped' sections do not require technical gear, but they will almost certainly induce the odd frisson, even in experienced hikers, and it goes without saying that if you don't like walking near drop-offs, or if exciting steps and airy ridges make your stomach churn, then this is probably a section you want to skip. It equally goes without saying (almost) that if children accompany you on these walks, they shouldn't be very young and they should be steady on their feet and protected where necessary. As for dogs – forget it!

These walks are generally long and strenuous and none of them should be attempted early in the summer season as remaining snow (névé) can make certain slopes extremely dicey.

# Classic Walks

 ## ROUTE 1
### *Mont Joly*

| | |
|---|---|
| **Start/Finish** | Pont de l'Ile 1000m |
| **Distance** | 10km |
| **Time** | 7hr |
| **Terrain** | Steep tracks and small paths, some of which can be muddy and some of which are very eroded near the summit. |
| **High point** | Mont Joly 2525m |
| **Altitude gain** | 1525m |
| **Map** | IGN Top 25 3531 OT Megève |
| **Parking** | Turn off the main road at a sign to La Chapelle. Follow the road around right to Les Hoches. Park at the bridge just beyond – Pont de l'Ile. |

Mont Joly is seen from so many places in the Arve valley that it goes without question that it must be a fine belvedere and indeed it is one of the best. It's almost true to say that what you can't see from here isn't worth seeing – close up are the Dômes de Miage and the Aiguilles de Tré-la-Tête, de Bionnassay, du Goûter and des Glaciers, Mont Blanc, of course, and beyond are the Beaufortain, Vanoise and Ecrins massifs.

Sadly, the walk itself isn't quite so prestigious as it takes wide tracks and small paths through an area largely sacrificed to skiing. However, the views really do make this route worthwhile, so enjoy the nice parts (notably some pleasant pastoral hamlets) and ignore the rest.

It is possible to continue on from the summit along the narrow ridge. However, the route as a there and back is already long enough for most people.

From the car park take the track signed to Pocherey, heading west. This leads up through meadows and soon arrives at the pretty hamlet of Le Carteyron. Don't be distracted here – it's very easy to miss the signpost indicating a steep four-wheel drive track which is signed to Pocherey and takes off from behind the chalets.

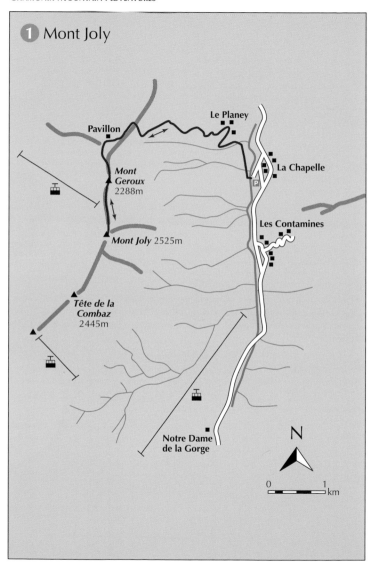

# ① Mont Joly

Le Planey

Pavillon

*Mont Geroux* 2288m

La Chapelle

*Mont Joly* 2525m

Les Contamines

▲ *Tête de la Combaz* 2445m

Notre Dame de la Gorge

N

0   1 km

*On the Mont Joly Ridge
(photo: Pete Marland)*

Keep following the track and eventually you'll reach the ridge that separates Les Contamines from Megève. ▶

Head up the ridge, at first on a good steep path, which becomes less worn after a path heads off rightwards. Stay on the small ridge path to a flat area where a wide track heads off right. Don't take this, go on to the top of a chairlift. Beyond this is a wooden hut and the path goes left of this up the ridge – it's not obvious until you get on it, but despite being very eroded there are some paint flashes and, although steep, it's still a proper path and soon it reaches the summit of **Mont Geroux** (2288m) on a nice flat and grassy ridge. This is a good place to catch your breath before continuing along the all too obvious ridge path to a final ascent to **Mont Joly** and its rather fine orientation table.

Return by the same route.

The immediate surroundings are rather compromised by ski lifts and associated junk, but lift your eyes and admire that fabulous view of the massif.

**ROUTE 2**

*Le Prarion*

| | |
|---|---|
| **Start/Finish** | La Côte 1131m |
| **Distance** | 5km to the cable car; 9km if the descent is done on foot |
| **Time** | 5hr 30min–6hr |
| **Terrain** | Good path all the way, with just a few sections near the ridge protected by hand-lines for those of a nervous disposition. |
| **High point** | Le Prarion 1969m |
| **Altitude gain** | 850m |
| **Map** | IGN Top 25 3531 ET Saint-Gervais-les-Bains |
| **Parking** | At La Côte. There is parking at the Amis de la Nature building, or just further up the road on the left. |
| **Note** | If you plan to take the lift down, then it might be best to park and start at the Prarion lift car park. In this case walk along the Route des Chavants to the Chemin des S'Nailles on the left. Go up this then onwards up the Chemin de Bovresse to emerge again on the Route des Chavants. From here follow signs right along the road to Charousse. |

Le Prarion is a peak that doesn't come close to attaining even half the height of most of the lofty summits that surround it, but as is so often the case with these small non-glaciated tops, it occupies a privileged position on the edge of the Mont Blanc massif and therefore offers superlative and wide-ranging views, making it one of the best belvederes in the Chamonix valley.

Now, you can get these views without all the sweat and toil of walking uphill by taking the Prarion cable car, but no walker would want to miss out on the wonderful and unlikely route to the Prarion summit (which is not where the lift goes to). Starting in Les Chavants the trail first takes you to the beautiful hamlet of Charousse, then the forested shade of the Col de la Forclaz and finally climbs the rugged summit ridge.

The lift offers the best descent option (especially for those with creaky knees).

From La Côte take the track through the beech forest to **Charousse** and take a few minutes to marvel at this perfect alpine hamlet. Continue onwards (signed to Col de la

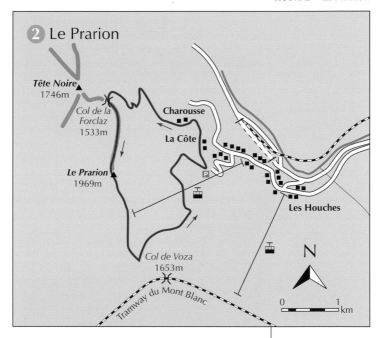

## 2 Le Prarion

Tête Noire
1746m

Col de la
Forclaz
1533m

Charousse

La Côte

Le Prarion
1969m

P

Les Houches

Col de Voza
1653m

Tramway du Mont Blanc

N

0          1
└───────┘ km

Forclaz) around the hillside under the shaly slopes of Le Prarion. After an easy track, the path on the right heads

*On the summit of Prarion*

up steeply in the woods to emerge onto another track and the **Col de la Forclaz** (1533m) is soon reached.

Now comes the real gem of the ascent – the trail up the broad north ridge of **Le Prarion**. At first views are tantalisingly brief as the path winds through forest, but once above the treeline the panorama is superb, alternately Mont Blanc, the Chamonix Aiguilles and the Aiguilles Rouges to the left, and the Arve valley and the Aravis range to the right. This excellent trail continues (occasionally protected by hand-line cables) through a carpet of alpenrose, past a small col to reach the long, rounded summit where the high point is marked by a cairn.

The descent path, clearly marked continuing along the ridge heading south, winds its way down through rocks and shrubs to the top of the **Prarion cable car**. Hop in to save the knees.

There are two options for descent on foot. The easiest option is to continue south-east along the signed trail to the Col de Voza. Before reaching the col, take the well-signed track down – preferably the one going towards Maison Neuve if you want to return to La Côte.

More direct, but less knee-friendly, is to descend under the ski drag-lift, which is between the Prarion cable car and the Prarion hotel/restaurant. Follow these grassy slopes all the way down to the top of the Maison Neuve lift where you'll join the track described above coming down from the Col de Voza. Turn left along the track. This leads all the way down to Les Houches, but to return to La Côte it's best to take a path that soon goes off left, signed to Les Baux/Charousse. This descends diagonally and very pleasantly through the woods to an unsigned junction with a mountain bike symbol for the right-hand way. You'll come out on the road at the Amis de la Nature building car park. To return to the cable car parking, go along the Route des Chavants, then turn left down the Chemin des Bovresse and continue along the Chemin des S'Nailles to meet the Route des Chavants again, which is followed rightwards to the car park.

# ROUTE 3
*Aiguillette des Houches*

| | |
|---|---|
| **Start/Finish** | Le Bettey 1340m |
| **Distance** | 10km |
| **Time** | 5hr 30min–6hr |
| **Terrain** | The trails are all good but the arête is airy and the descent begins steeply. |
| **High point** | Aiguillette des Houches 2285m |
| **Altitude gain** | 950m |
| **Map** | IGN Top 25 3531 ET Saint-Gervais-les-Bains |
| **Parking** | Le Bettey, on the road from Le Coupeau to La Flatière |

The Aiguillette des Houches, 2285m, forms part of the wonderful curved ridgeline that defines the southern end of the Aiguilles Rouges range before it plunges into the deep ravine of the Diosaz Gorge. It is situated at the far end of the Chamonix valley and enjoys uninterrupted views of Mont Blanc and associated glacial splendour, as well as the more distant limestone massifs – the Aravis and the Rocher des Fiz/Anterne.

There are various routes to reach the summit and the one described here is reasonably arduous as it traverses the summit without taking advantage of the relatively nearby Brévent lift system. By going this way you can include the delightfully airy Pierre Blanche ridge, which adds a certain zest to the hike.

From Le Bettey go along the road towards **La Flatière** and be sure to look at the view from this idyllic spot. A path heads off right to **Plan de la Cry** signed as 'Plan de la Cry par sentier'. Take this. The Pierre Blanche is signed left soon after and later left again. This trail goes north across a wooded hillside in a rising traverse. At a junction (straight ahead, signed to Montvauthier) go right up a pleasant trail in the woods. ▶

This path takes you to the **Pierre Blanche** ridge at Pt 1687 on the IGN Top 25 map.

There is a light-coloured rock by the trail – is this the Pierre Blanche?

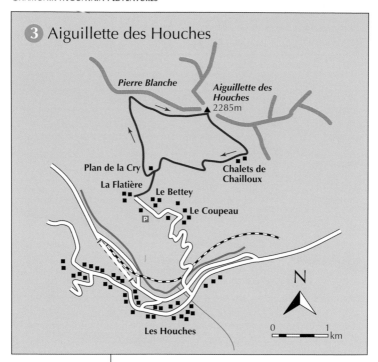

**3** Aiguillette des Houches

*Pierre Blanche*

*Aiguillette des Houches*
2285m

Plan de la Cry

La Flatière

Le Bettey

**Chalets de Chailloux**

Le Coupeau

Les Houches

N

0    1
km

Now the shoulder is followed, with extensive views down to the Diosaz Gorge on one side and towards the Mont Blanc massif on the other. The ridge leads to the summit of **Aiguillette des Houches**, with just one detour to the right (southern slopes) under the first high point.

Once on the summit enjoy that 360° vista – this is a really special panorama.

For the descent, head south in a series tight of zig-zags, which soon give way to easier ground. Pleasant high meadows are descended to reach a sharp turn right (west) to the **Chalets de Chailloux**, where there will most likely be a big flock of sheep grazing. After the chalets the path goes into forest. At the path junction at 1782m choose the right-hand option signed to Plan de la Cry,

which goes down to this hamlet. A quick descent past the houses and you'll be back at the car.

*High above the sea of cloud in the Arve valley, on the Aiguillette des Houches*

# 🚶 ROUTE 4
### Montagne de la Côte

| | |
|---|---|
| **Start** | Chalet du Glacier des Bossons 1350m (or the base of the chairlift 1020m) |
| **Finish** | Base of the chairlift 1020m |
| **Distance** | 9.25km |
| **Time** | 6hr 30min–7hr |
| **Terrain** | Good path all the way, but can remain snowy higher up. There are a couple of sections of very easy scrambling. |
| **High point** | Junction of the Montagne de la Côte and the Bossons Glacier 2589m |
| **Altitude gain** | 1240m |
| **Map** | IGN Top 25 3531 ET Saint-Gervais-les-Bains |
| **Parking** | Near Le Mont at the base of the chairlift going up to the Chalet du Glacier des Bossons known as the Télésiège du Glacier. |

The Bossons Glacier – 7.8km long with an average slope of 45° from its source near the summit of Mont Blanc – snakes down to the Chamonix valley, allegedly making the biggest vertical drop of any glacier anywhere. This frozen river moves at the relatively rapid rate of 250m a year and if you fall into a crevasse near the top, you might pop out at the bottom between 25 and 40 years later.

The Montagne de la Côte is the ridge that runs between the Bossons Glacier and the much less impressive Taconnaz Glacier, and from the ridge you'll get fantastic views of the teetering icy pinnacles and walls that make up the lower part of the glacier.

This glacier (like almost all glaciers) is retreating and the melt has been impressive over the last 100 years. Even so, the seracs and icy walls are spectacular seen from above, and this is largely due to the steepness of the glacier, making it more chaotic than most flatter glaciers.

At the top of the ridge you are confronted by a sea of ice – La Jonction – which is where the Bossons and Taconnaz Glaciers go their separate ways in descent, and the panorama is exceptional. The Refuge des Grands Mulets is just visible on a rocky ridge ahead, beyond which seemingly interminable swathes of ice lead to the far-off summit of Mont Blanc.

This walk is about more than glacial scenery, impressive though it is. It's a walk in the footsteps of the **first ascensionists** of Mont Blanc itself. Back in the late 18th century a race was on to find a way to reach this seemingly impossible summit and in 1786 Jacques Balmat and Gabriel Paccard finally made their apprehensive way up this ridge to get onto the glacier, from where they eventually found the key to success. They bivvied at the top of the ridge under a couple of huge boulders, now known as the Gîte à Balmat, just before ground gives way to ice, and one can only imagine their trepidation as they dined on red wine and tough bread, wondering what the next day held in store for them.

Taking the chairlift is recommended as it avoids an additional 300m of ascent and delivers you at the **Chalet du Glacier des Bossons**. Already the views of the Bossons

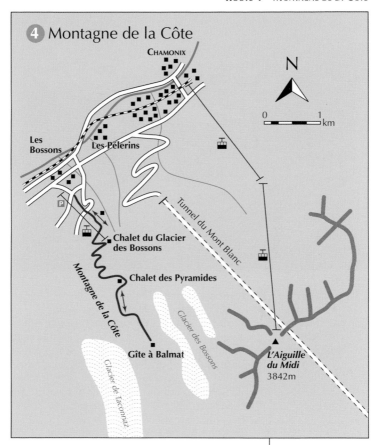

Glacier are impressive. It's worth taking the time to check out the fascinating artefacts gathered at the hut, which were collected from the glacier after two Air India crashes on the summit of Mont Blanc in 1950 and 1966. There are also interesting photos showing the regression of the glacier over the years.

A wide trail goes on up to the **Chalet des Pyramides** (1895m) and takes about an hour. Just below the café

*The Montagne de la Côte is the ridge on the left, between the Bossons Glacier and the Taconnaz Glacier*

there are fine views of the seracs far below, with an imposing view of the Aiguille Verte as backdrop.

From here onwards the path isn't so wide or frequented, but it is well marked, snaking up between one ridge and the other: one minute you're enjoying views of the Taconnaz Glacier and Mont Blanc, next minute looking up the Chamonix valley towards the Col de Balme.

A couple of hours after Les Pyramides you reach the **Gîte à Balmat** (2530m) and then it's a short 50m climb to the end of the ridge and the start of the ice.

Descend by the same route, continuing all the way down the footpath from the Chalet du Glacier des Bossons, unless you want to hop on the lift again and save your knees.

**ROUTE 5**

*Lac Cornu and Lacs Noirs*

| | |
|---|---|
| **Start** | Top of Index lift 2385m |
| **Finish** | Planpraz 2000m |
| **Distance** | 6.3km |
| **Time** | 3hr 30min–4hr (this doesn't include the descent to Lac Cornu or the lower Lac Noir) |
| **Terrain** | The trails are all good, if a little bouldery, and there is just one section of very easy cable. |
| **High point** | Lac Noirs 2500m |
| **Altitude gain** | Approximately 200m, more if you descend to Lac Cornu and/ or the lower Lac Noir |
| **Map** | IGN Top 25 3630 OT Chamonix Mont Blanc |
| **Parking** | La Flégère cable car, Les Praz |

While the south side of the Aiguilles Rouges is incredibly and justifiably popular, once over on the north side you enter a wilderness area where rocky buttresses shield hidden lakes and corries and all around are mountains and deep valleys.

Lacs Cornu and Noirs give the best of both worlds, being accessible from either the Planpraz or Flégère lift systems, but situated on the wild side of the range. The best way to do this walk is to start at one lift and finish at the other. The walk can be done in either direction and is described here starting at La Flégère and finishing at the Brévent.

The lakes provide good swimming for those hardy souls willing to take the plunge, while others will prefer to sit on the rocky beaches savouring the views away towards the Rochers des Fiz and the hazy depths of the Arve valley.

Take the cable car to La Flégère and then the Index chair-lift. A trail leads off to the left (south-west) to the edge of the large corries formed by the Aiguille de la Glière and the Aiguille Pourrie. Follow this down a rounded ridge to a small col (2361m), then pick up the good path across the corries to the **Col de la Glière** at 2461m. A short section of cable assists as the col is reached.

# 5 Lac Cornu and Lacs Noirs

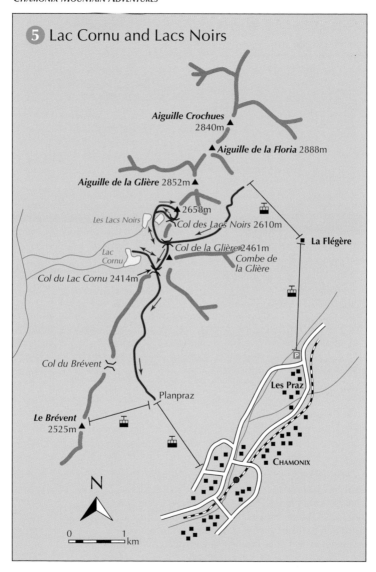

*Aiguille Crochues* 2840m

▲ *Aiguille de la Floria* 2888m

*Aiguille de la Glière* 2852m ▲

2658m

*Les Lacs Noirs*

*Col des Lacs Noirs* 2610m

■ **La Flégère**

*Lac Cornu*

*Col de la Glière* 2461m

*Combe de la Glière*

*Col du Lac Cornu* 2414m

*Col du Brévent* ⟩⟨

Planpraz

**Les Praz**

*Le Brévent* 2525m ▲

**CHAMONIX**

N

0    1 km

*Lac Cornu with the Rochers des Fiz behind*

From here the path continues south above the Lac Cornu, but it would be a great shame to miss out on the Lacs Noirs. To reach these beautiful lakes you need to follow yellow waymarks up towards the right (north) along a rocky ridge – the first lake is reached in about 20min. Continue following the waymarks and the next lake is to be found further down and on the left. ▸

*By now, if it's hot, you'll be ready for a stop and a dip.*

To continue with the route to Lac Cornu, return to the Col de la Glière then follow the rocky trail south to the **Col du Lac Cornu** (2414m). The going is a bit rough but never difficult or exposed. Views down to the lake and beyond to the Rochers des Fiz are spectacular.

At the col a red waymarked path heads right (west) to the Lac Cornu. You might decide to descend to the lakes, but keep your eye on the time as you don't want to miss the last lift down from **Planpraz**. To reach this cable car a good path goes south, taking about 1hr.

**Extension**

To extend the walk, from the higher Lac Noir head northwards to a small col on the ridge above the lake. A sparsely cairned route leads right (east) up light-coloured rock, with a little easy scrambling, to an unnamed **summit** at 2685m perched high above the Chamonix valley with the Mer de Glace directly opposite. Cairns go down via the **Col des Lacs Noirs** and back to the

first lake. This extension is more difficult than the rest
of the walk.

 **ROUTE 6**

*Plan de l'Aiguille to Montenvers*

| | |
|---|---|
| **Start** | Plan de l'Aiguille 2310m |
| **Finish** | Chamonix 1037m |
| **Distance** | 5km from Plan de l'Aiguille to Montenvers; 10km all the way to Chamonix |
| **Time** | 4hr (not including time to visit sites at Montenvers); 2hr if you choose to descend by train |
| **Terrain** | Good paths but in very bad weather the traverse from the Plan de l'Aiguille to Montenvers may demand some concentration as the rocky ground could be slippery, and early in the season this traverse should be avoided as névé is probable. |
| **High point** | Plan de l'Aiguille 2310m |
| **Altitude gain** | 120m |
| **Map** | IGN Top 25 3630 OT Chamonix Mont Blanc |
| **Parking** | The Aiguille du Midi cable car |

A small train runs from Chamonix to Montenvers, but a much more
interesting and scenic approach is to be had along the Grand Balcon Nord
trail from the midway station of the Aiguille du Midi cable car. This path
takes an undulating traverse all the way to Montenvers and you can add
a little extra by going up to the spectacular viewpoint of Signal Forbes just
before reaching Montenvers itself.

Once at Montenvers various delights await, apart from the views: the
hotel has its own restaurant and is worth a visit if only to relive the journey
of Victorian travellers who would make their way up there on mules; there
is also a small museum and a crystal display and, for as long as it lasts,
the Grotte de Glace (ice-cave), which becomes more and more difficult to
maintain as the glacier shunts and loses depth. From Montenvers you might
walk down the old mule track back to Chamonix or alternatively save the
knees and take the train.

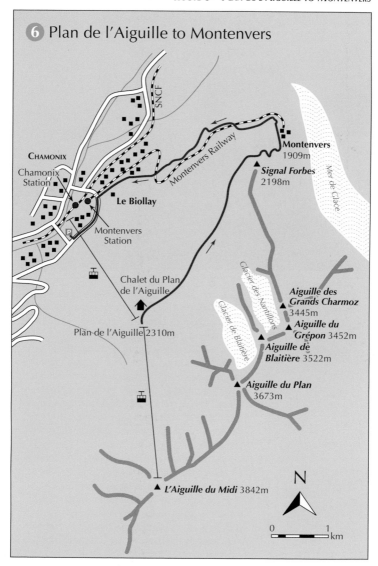

# 6 Plan de l'Aiguille to Montenvers

SNCF

Montenvers Railway

**Montenvers**
1909m

*Mer de Glace*

**CHAMONIX**

Chamonix Station

**Le Biollay**

▲ *Signal Forbes*
*2198m*

Montenvers Station

Chalet du Plan de l'Aiguille

Plan-de l'Aiguille 2310m

*Glacier des Nantillons*

*Aiguille des Grands Charmoz*
*3445m*

*Glacier de Blaitière*

*Aiguille du Grépon 3452m*

*Aiguille de Blaitière 3522m*

▲ *Aiguille du Plan*
*3673m*

▲ *L'Aiguille du Midi* 3842m

N

0        1
▬▬▬▬▬▬km

65

*Sam taking a break on the way to the Signal Forbes (photo: Roger Portch)*

In the 18th century the **Mer de Glace Glacier** was truly a sight to behold. This was what the early travellers to the Alps came to see – a huge crevasse-ridden sea of ice stretching all the way down to the valley in one massive tongue. At this time there was what is now known as the Little Ice Age, a period of time when the glaciers grew and were pushing down into the valleys, right up against people's houses. People were so intimidated by these huge and powerful forces that they would call in the priest to exorcise the spirits thought to be embodied in these frozen rivers.

To the well-heeled tourists doing their obligatory European Tour, the glacier had to be visited, usually on the back of a mule, guided by locals. Once at Montenvers these wealthy visitors would stay at the Montenvers Hotel and attempt to traverse the glacier – photos abound of ladies in crinolines being assisted across gaping crevasses by their attentive guides.

Nowadays the glacier is but a shadow of its former self and each year loses many metres from its snout. However, it's still worth a visit and Montenvers, site of an old hotel, gives the best views both of the ice and also the surrounding mighty peaks, notably the Drus.

It is a sobering thought that not so long ago local farmers would take their cows across the glacier from Montenvers to graze on the slopes under the Drus. Now many metres of gravel moraine separate the top of the glacier from the grass under the Drus.

Leave the cable car station and take the trail down to the **Chalet du Plan de l'Aiguille**. The path onwards is clearly signed across the hillside, in and out of gullies and around boulders, holding steady to the 2100m contour line. Do concentrate though. Lots of smaller trails head off upwards, formed by climbers accessing the big granite needles above.

A little less than an hour from the chalet a path heads off right to the **Signal Forbes**, named after James Forbes, a Scottish geologist in the 19th century. Take this and climb up to a flat area decorated with cairns. This is the Signal (2198m) and is one of the few places from where you can see the famous North Face of the Grandes Jorasses. A good paved trail leads down to **Montenvers** arriving at the Temple de la Nature, one of the first buildings to be constructed here in the 19th century – this now houses the museum.

The descent path starts just next to the hotel. The best way is marked on the map as the Chemin du Montenvers, which was the old mule track before the railway was built, and goes past the Buvette Caillet, exiting the forest at Les Planards. For the childlike at heart there is then the option of making the final descent to **Le Biollay** on the summer luge! Walk along the road back to the Midi car park.

If you don't want to walk down, you could hop on the train from Montenvers to Chamonix.

# ROUTE 7

*Grand Balcon Sud:*
*La Flégère to Planpraz*

| | |
|---|---|
| **Start** | Chalet de la Flégère 1871m |
| **Finish** | Planpraz 2000m |
| **Distance** | 5km |
| **Time** | 2hr |
| **Terrain** | Good trail all the way, easy to find. Some slightly narrow sections might not be appreciated by those with a true fear of drops. |
| **High point** | Planpraz 2000m |
| **Altitude gain** | 200m |
| **Map** | IGN Top 25 3630 OT Chamonix Mont Blanc |
| **Parking** | La Flégère cable car, Les Praz |

This walk perhaps could rate as the most scenic walk in the Chamonix valley. While it isn't long, the views it affords are quite simply unbeatable, spanning the whole of the glaciated range, from the Aiguille Verte at the north end to Mont Blanc and the Aiguille du Goûter further south.

The Grand Balcon trails Nord and Sud are two of four balcony routes that exist in the valley. The Petit Balcon Nord and Sud stay at valley level, whereas the Grand Balcons are generally above the treeline. This walk takes part of the trail on the south side of the valley, right opposite the Mont Blanc massif. It can be lengthened in various ways, but as it is described here it will occupy you for a couple of hours or longer, depending on how long you choose to savour those vistas.

Unlike most walks in the Alps, this one is fairly flat. It starts at the top of La Flégère cable car and more or less hugs the 2000m contour line all the way around to the Planpraz cable car, with the odd undulation thrown in just to keep you on your toes.

Take the cable car up to **La Flégère**. Descend to the **Chalet de la Flégère** (mountain hut and café situated just below) and pick up the trail heading right (south-west).

# ⑦ Grand Balcon Sud: La Flégère to Planpraz

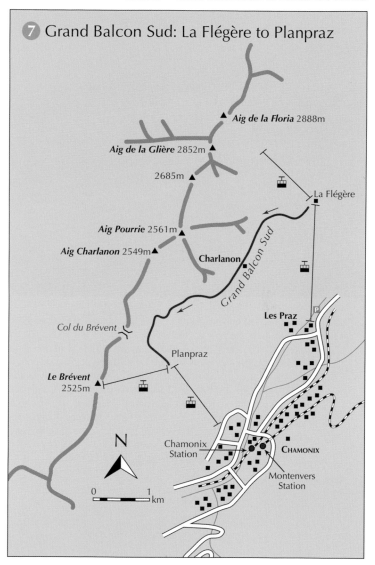

*Aig de la Floria* 2888m ▲

*Aig de la Glière* 2852m ▲

2685m ▲

*Aig Pourrie* 2561m ▲

*Aig Charlanon* 2549m ▲

**Charlanon**

La Flégère

*Grand Balcon Sud*

*Col du Brévent*

**Les Praz**

Planpraz

*Le Brévent* 2525m ▲

N

Chamonix Station

**CHAMONIX**

Montenvers Station

0     1 km

*The Grand Balcon Sud offers superlative views of Mont Blanc, here with a foreground of alpenrose*

In early summer the trail is bordered by pink flowering alpenrose, while later in the season bilberries will tempt you to stop and graze.

The trail is signed to Planpraz – be careful not to descend on the track to Les Praz. ◄

The path winds around the hillside with one short but steep staircase and some slightly narrow sections – take care when passing hikers coming the other way. The open meadows of **Charlanon** provide a nice place to stop and there is even a fountain here but don't rely on it as it may be dry in late summer. Enjoy this beautiful spot, for soon after you'll reach the ugly ski slopes of **Le Brévent**. Once at **Planpraz** you might be lucky enough to see the paragliders taking off just above the lift station.

**ROUTE 8**

*Aiguillette des Posettes*

| | |
|---|---|
| **Start/Finish** | Car park just before the Col des Montets 1430m |
| **Distance** | 10.2km |
| **Time** | 5hr 30min–6hr |
| **Terrain** | The trails range from very easy tracks to regular mountain paths. |
| **High point** | Aiguillette des Posettes 2201m |
| **Altitude gain** | 930m |
| **Map** | IGN Top 25 3630 OT Chamonix Mont Blanc |
| **Parking** | South side of the Col des Montets, on the right when coming from Chamonix, just after Tré-le-Champ |

Situated at the head of the Chamonix valley, the Aiguillette des Posettes not surprisingly is blessed with superb views. It also has various other attributes that make it one of the best non-glaciated peaks in the region. Firstly, the route to the top is varied, starting in forest then emerging above the treeline on a fine rounded ridge with views on both sides; secondly, there are a couple of cable cars nearby, which can be used to aid the descent or indeed the ascent if desired; lastly, it's easy to traverse the summit, descending by a different route to make a round trip of it.

From the car park the trail heads east into the forest and wends its way up north-east. All junctions are signed to the Aiguillette des Posettes. At an obvious clearing a sign points left for the 'Aiguillette via la crête' – take this. The path zigzags up to a rockier section where steep steps are interspersed with flatter grassy sections and a couple of small tarns provide marshy ground for cotton grass and orchids to grow. ▶

The views open up to the south as well as to either side of the ridge.

There are several false summits but the true one, **Aiguillette des Posettes** at 2201m, is unmistakable with its huge cairn. The panoramic view includes the whole of

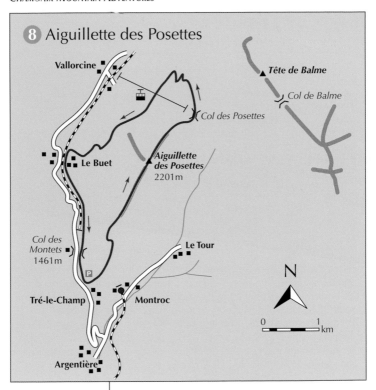

# ⑧ Aiguillette des Posettes

Vallorcine

Tête de Balme

Col de Balme

Col des Posettes

Le Buet

**Aiguillette des Posettes**
2201m

Col des
Montets
1461m

Le Tour

Tré-le-Champ

Montroc

N

0 —————— 1 km

Argentière

the Mont Blanc massif on the east side of the Chamonix valley, the Aiguilles Rouges to the west, Mont Buet (rarely seen so well) and the Lac d'Emosson. Beyond are the Dent de Morcles and the Swiss Rhône valley stretching all the way to the Bernese Alps.

To descend take the good trail that continues northeast to the **Col des Posettes** (1997m). Here head down past the top of the **Vallorcine cable car** (an alternative means of descent) and stay on the wide track until a turn off to the left is found, signed to Le Buet/Vallorcine. This leads down through the forest to the Vallorcine valley. At a junction turn left towards **Le Buet** and stay on the left of

the railway line on the Chemin des Diligences to return to the **Col des Montets** (1461m). From the col the Sentier Botanique gives an interesting end to the walk, right back to the car park.

*The summit of the Aiguillette des Posettes gives the full 360° vista*

 **ROUTE 9**

*Lac Blanc from the Col des Montets*

| | |
|---|---|
| **Start** | Col des Montets 1461m |
| **Finish** | La Flégère cable car 1871m |
| **Distance** | 7.25km (assuming public transport is used to get back from the lift station to the car park) |
| **Time** | 5hr |
| **Terrain** | The trails are all fairly good, if a little stony at times. There is a short cabled section with an easy ladder just before the hut. |
| **High point** | Lac Blanc 2352m |
| **Altitude gain** | 900m |
| **Map** | IGN Top 25 3630 OT Chamonix Mont Blanc |
| **Parking** | At the Col des Montets itself, opposite the Chalet de la Réserve |

Lac Blanc, with its eponymous hut, has to be a contender for 'most famous walking objective in the Chamonix Valley' and justifiably so; for not only are the views unsurpassable, it is also very easy to get to, being just a 1hr 30min walk from the top of the Flégère cable car.

However, Lac Blanc can also be approached from the other direction (north), starting at the Col des Montets road pass, and this hike is far more strenuous and varied. Going up this way then taking the main trail to the lift for the descent is a great way to visit this wonderful viewpoint, giving a good mountain day.

The route is at first quite steep, but well graded. Once the initial 800m of ascent are achieved, you're rewarded with the tempting clear water of the Chéserys Lakes. Those of a hardy disposition may well take a dip here, but be prepared for a shock – even on a hot day the water is bracing! The final part of the ascent to the hut has some cable-aided sections but they are short-lived and not difficult.

This walk actually has a sign and a map devoted to it at the Col des Montets and is called 'Le Sentier des Lacs de Montagne'. There are some information signs alongside the ascent.

Leave the car park, cross the road and take the all too obvious zigzag path that wends its unrelenting way up the hillside to **La Remuaz**. En route there are a couple of good resting places on flatter rocky areas, but basically this is a head down and get on with it job. Once the main climb is done you'll be able to appreciate the great views of the massif and the valley below. There will almost certainly be ibex watching your pain as you ascend.

Once the terrain flattens, the way is very pleasant, among rocks and vegetation to the inviting **Lacs des Chéserys**. Here other walkers will most likely join your route, having come up from Argentière. Be careful to stay on the higher path to **Lac Blanc**, not to be led astray on the big trail that goes directly to La Flégère. Although the path is well made it would be easy to lose the way at this point in foggy conditions. To reach the hut you'll need to ascend some easy equipped sections of trail, which can create some traffic jams in high season.

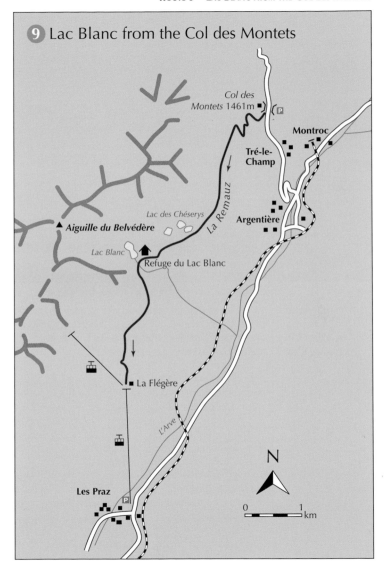

**9** Lac Blanc from the Col des Montets

Col des Montets 1461m

Montroc

Tré-le-Champ

La Remauz

Lac des Chéserys

Argentière

▲ *Aiguille du Belvédère*

*Lac Blanc*

Refuge du Lac Blanc

La Flégère

*L'Arve*

**Les Praz**

N

0        1 km

*Ibex next to the path on the trail from Remuaz*

Note that the Refuge du Lac Blanc is also known as the Chalet du Lac Blanc.

At the **Refuge du Lac Blanc** take the time to wander by the lakes and also, of course, to take refreshments on the terrace. The old hut is nearby – this was destroyed by avalanche some years ago. ◄

To descend, take the good path south from the hut. This is well signed all the way and provides a very pleasant return route to the **La Flégère cable car station** at 1871m. The last lift down is usually around 5.00 or 5.30pm and in high season there will often be a queue. Walking down is certainly an option, but the trail joins ski pistes from time to time, which are not knee-friendly. It takes an extra 1hr 30min to descend on foot.

Once down at **Les Praz** you can take the Chamonix Bus back to the Col des Montets, or the train to Montroc where a nice trail wanders around via Tré-le-Champ to get back to the col.

**ROUTE 10**

*Mont Buet by the Normal Route*

| | |
|---|---|
| **Start/Finish** | Le Buet 1350m |
| **Distance** | 20km |
| **Time** | 1hr 30min to the hut; 8hr round trip next day |
| **Terrain** | The path to the hut is excellent. Onwards, the trail to the summit can be indistinct, especially if there is late névé which can persist the whole summer on shady slopes. Don't go early in the season or the snow will probably be too deep to walk on. |
| **High point** | Mont Buet 3096m |
| **Altitude gain** | 576m to the Refuge Pierre à Bérard; 1170m from there to the summit |
| **Map** | IGN Top 25 3630 OT Chamonix Mont Blanc |
| **Parking** | Le Buet railway station |

Mont Buet, at 3096m, is the highest peak in the Aiguilles Rouges range. It enjoys something of a reputation locally, long regarded as a challenging training walk for those with their sights set on the glaciated side of the valley – the so-called 'Normal' Route should not be underestimated with its 1746m of ascent and descent!

The effort of the climb is amply rewarded as the summit provides a fantastic grandstand from where to view the whole area, from the Mont Blanc massif to the nearer Valais peaks in Switzerland, as well as the limestone valleys and peaks of the Giffre and the Aravis ranges.

The route can certainly be done in a day from Le Buet, but unless you're looking for a humdinger of an outing it is best divided into a two-day trip, with a night spent at the Refuge Pierre à Bérard. Then you get to do the steepest part of the ascent in the cool of the morning and still be in a fit state for the descent – which will feel mighty long whether you've stayed at the hut or not. A beer on the way down tends to help.

Follow the route from Le Buet up to the **Refuge de la Pierre à Bérard**, described in Hut Walks, Route 7. From the hut the trail is signed and heads to the right up the grassy and rocky hillside in a series of good zigzags. The

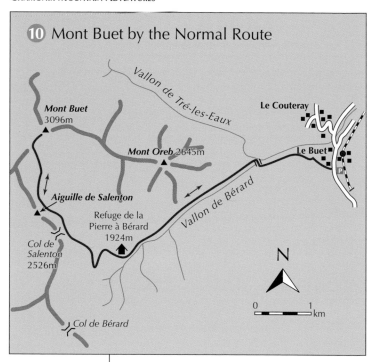

### 10 Mont Buet by the Normal Route

Vallon de Tré-les-Eaux

**Mont Buet**
3096m

Le Couteray

**Mont Oreb** 2645m

Le Buet

*Aiguille de Salenton*

Vallon de Bérard

Refuge de la
Pierre à Bérard
1924m

*Col de
Salenton*
2526m

N

0       1
└────┴────┘km

*Col de Bérard*

way soon leads round to the left and up into an area of
orange rocks under the **Col de Salenton** (2526m) – there
are waymarks but they are easily missed. A traverse leads
under the Aiguille de Salenton and arrives eventually at a
small col, from where you can see the way to the summit
– so hope is restored.

Continue to climb in steady zigzags until a traverse
right under a small summit where there is an aerial. The
map shows an *abri* (shelter) in this area but it's extremely
small, old and easy to miss. Not something to rely on in
case of bad weather.

Eventually you emerge onto the Arête de Mortine and
this rounded shoulder gives a fine end to the climb as the
angle is kind and the panorama exactly what you've been

*On the ascent to Mont Buet, looking down to the Villy valley*

dreaming of. To the north and west are the Giffre valley and the Anterne plateau; to the east and south the Mont Blanc massif; and just up ahead the summit of **Mont Buet** (3096m), with its big cairn and almost certainly lots of other hikers celebrating their ascent. ▶

Return by the same route.

In true French machismo style it is also known locally as le Mont Blanc des dames!

# Family Walks

 **ROUTE 1**
*Lacs des Ilettes*

| | |
|---|---|
| **Start/Finish** | Lac des Ilettes 530m |
| **Distance** | 5.5km |
| **Time** | 2hr |
| **Terrain** | The trails are good in general but can be a little muddy after heavy rain. The first lake has a supervised swimming area plus another that is not supervised. The second lake is reserved for sailing and windsurfing. |
| **Altitude gain** | 0m or thereabouts |
| **Map** | Top 25 3530 OT Cluses Sallanches |
| **Parking** | Lacs des Ilettes, Saint-Martin, on the far side of the Arve from Sallanches. The road to Saint-Martin leaves the main road from Chedde to Sallanches just before the roundabout at the start of the *zone industrielle* on the right and is signed 'Vieux Pont Saint Martin, Lacs des Ilettes, Cascade d'Arpenaz'. Go through Saint-Martin-sur-Arve and keep going, straight ahead at a three-way junction with a stop sign, signed 'Lacs des Ilettes'. You'll pass the old aerodrome on the left, then you'll see the first lake on the left, where a big car park is entered under a wooden gateway. |
| **Note** | Dogs allowed |

The Lacs des Ilettes are two lakes down in the Arve valley, on the northern edge of Sallanches. This is a very useful walk for a bad weather day or if you want to go shopping down in Sallanches, but could also give a restful day in good weather as the views are stunning (the Mont Blanc massif looks quite different from this perspective) and the lakeside provides a great vantage point for the Aravis peaks, which tower above the Arve valley. In addition, the grassy shoreline tempts with some delightful picnic spots and in the summer it's usually warm enough for a dip. A really welcome change after days spent in the mountains, or for those high season days mid-August when Chamonix is a heaving mass of flesh.

This walk makes a circuit of the lakes, with the added objective of the Cascade d'Arpenaz, which after heavy rain is an impressive waterfall pouring down limestone cliffs beyond the lakes. It's a walk for everyone and the trails are good enough for bikes and pushchairs.

Most visitors driving to Chamonix just get onto the Autoroute Blanche and bypass **Sallanches**, thinking there is nothing of interest there. In fact, Sallanches is quite attractive and has a pleasant town centre with a landscaped central area and very nice riverside cafés near the tourist office. It's also worth visiting the Chateau des Rubins, which is a beautiful old

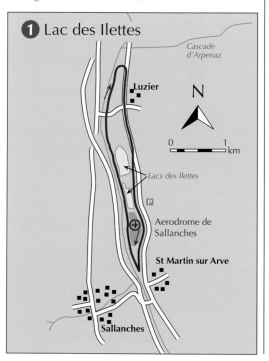

**① Lac des Ilettes**

Cascade d'Arpenaz

Luzier

N

0     1 km

Lacs des Ilettes

P

Aerodrome de Sallanches

St Martin sur Arve

Sallanches

*The beach scene at the Lac des Ilettes*

castle with an excellent display of alpine wildlife and geology.

Go back out onto the road and walk towards **Saint-Martin** (south) past the old **aerodrome** and past some new-build houses. Just before the crossroads at Saint-Martin, go right towards the river, signed 'Cascade d'Arpenaz 1hr 05'. The path heads to the river then runs parallel to it, in the trees. This takes you northwards past both lakes. After the second lake keep going, over a dry river bed.

The road provides a shortcut if needed.

This leads to a road then a trail heads left, signed again to the cascade. ◄

The continuation path is narrower and goes along-side a field. The Cascade de l'Arpenaz is the sometimes big waterfall cascading down cliffs ahead and on the right. Once you are opposite this, the trail leads right-wards and into the trees, until exiting the forest on a small road just before **Luzier** village, right opposite the water-fall. You can go up to the waterfall on the far side of the road.

To complete the circuit turn right and follow the road all the way back to the lakes. Although this section is road walking, there are not usually too many vehicles and the terrain is pleasant with grassy meadows and wildflowers all around. If you want to avoid the road take the signed path from the waterfall and this brings you out at the lakes.

# ROUTE 2

*Lacs Jovet*

| | |
|---|---|
| **Start/Finish** | Notre Dame de la Gorge 1210m |
| **Distance** | 14km |
| **Time** | 6hr |
| **Terrain** | Trails range from jeep track to stony trail |
| **Altitude gain** | 964m |
| **Map** | Top 25 3531 ET Saint-Gervais-les-Bains |
| **Parking** | Notre Dame de la Gorge, just outside Les Contamines-Montjoie |
| **Note** | No dogs allowed – Réserve Naturelle des Contamines-Montjoie |

A lake is always a delightful objective for a walk and the two Lacs Jovet at 2174m are no exception. Situated in a grandiose and wild cirque under the rocky summits of Mont Tondu and the Pain du Sucre, and right next to the Monts Jovet peaks, these lakes are surrounded by spectacular scenery. The way is quite long and the ascent considerable, but it's well broken up by flatter sections and it's possible to shorten the walk by only going as far as the Chalet de la Balme (marked on the map as La Balme Chalet Hôtel).

The lakes are just off the Tour of Mont Blanc trek and the first part of this walk coincides with that long-distance hike, so you'll be accompanied some of the way by heavily loaded hikers. However, you'll leave them as you head off from the main trail to the lakes.

Much of this walk is steeped in history, taking as it does the Roman Road, which heads arrow straight out of the Contamines valley.

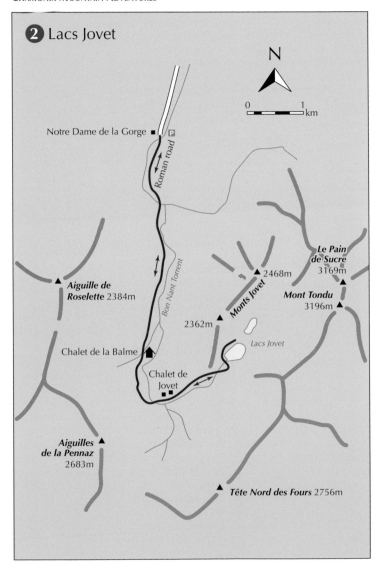

**2** Lacs Jovet

N

0    1 km

Notre Dame de la Gorge ■  🅿

Roman road

Bon Nant Torrent

▲ **Aiguille de Roselette** 2384m

▲ 2468m

*Monts Jovet*

*Le Pain de Sucre* 3169m ▲

*Mont Tondu* 3196m ▲

2362m

*Lacs Jovet*

Chalet de la Balme

Chalet de Jovet
■ ■

▲ **Aiguilles de la Pennaz** 2683m

▲ **Tête Nord des Fours** 2756m

The **Romans** descended this way as they headed through the Tarentaise en route from Italy, but they were certainly not the first. The Col de Bonhomme, beyond the Lacs Jovet, has served as a major route over the Alps for centuries and the Notre Dame de la Gorge chapel at the beginning of this walk is testament to the legions of travellers who have had to make what was once regarded as a very perilous journey. Long before the current chapel was built, there was a place of prayer at Notre Dame de la Gorge. The Roman Road runs above the deep and gloomy Bon Nant gorge with its gushing river and water-gouged walls. Along the way you'll find engravings marking the passing of long-forgotten travellers and the rocks of the trail are polished by the passage of many weary feet.

▶ From the car park head up the road to the chapel. The **Roman Road** starts here and begins very steeply. It lets up from time to time but should be taken slowly. There's plenty to look at – the age-old graffiti on the rocks and the occasional views down to the river provide diversions. Some way up the track there is a sign to a *pont naturel* (natural bridge), which can be viewed by descending to a small lookout. Higher up at a bridge there is a little path around to the left, which gives scary views down into the swirling waters of the gorge.

The name 'Jovet' is thought to be a derivative of the Roman name for Jupiter who was worshipped in Roman times.

Soon after there is a café on the left, followed by the Nant Borrant gîte and café on the right. The track eventually flattens out to give a very pleasant stretch past meadows and the odd chalet up to the **Chalet de la Balme**, which also sells drinks. The views open up and rocky peaks are seen all around. La Balme is a good objective in itself and if anyone is tiring then don't go on as it's a long way back.

Beyond the refuge a rough stony path is signed on the left to the Col du Bonhomme and Lacs Jovet. This climbs up quite steeply to a huge pylon. Continue along the trail to a flat area where marmots are often to be seen playing among the boulders. Here you'll leave the TMB trail to go east. The **Chalets de Jovet** are soon passed, then after a gentle ascent up pleasant slopes there is a final steeper climb to reach the beautiful **lakes**.

The return is by the same route, probably interspersed by café stops as it's a long way.

 **ROUTE 3**

*Chalets de Miage and Truc*

| | |
|---|---|
| **Start/Finish** | La Gruvaz 1150m |
| **Distance** | 7km |
| **Time** | 4–5hr round trip |
| **Terrain** | Good paths and tracks |
| **Altitude gain** | 570m |
| **Map** | Top 25 3531 ET Saint-Gervais-les-Bains |
| **Parking** | La Gruvaz |
| **Note** | Dogs allowed, but there will be cattle and/or sheep so they should be kept on a lead. |

The Miage cirque is one of the hidden joys of the Contamines valley. Forming the south-western flank of the Mont Blanc massif, the Dômes de Miage are somewhat lesser-known peaks, not visible from the main Chamonix valley. The cirque is tucked away under the glaciated faces of the Dômes and the Aiguille de Bionnassay, and is a real gem to visit.

The Chalet de Miage is a working farm but also a mountain refuge and restaurant, and lunch here on a sunny day in the garden is unforgettable, with a backdrop of the myriad ice sculptures of the nearby mountains. The Chalet du Truc is just a short climb above and also offers refreshments. It seems to be slightly quieter than the Miage Chalet.

From **La Gruvaz** go across the bridge and up into the woods on a wide track. The track leads in 1km or so to **Maison Neuve** at 1290m, a cluster of buildings in a clearing. Soon after this a junction is reached. Go left and

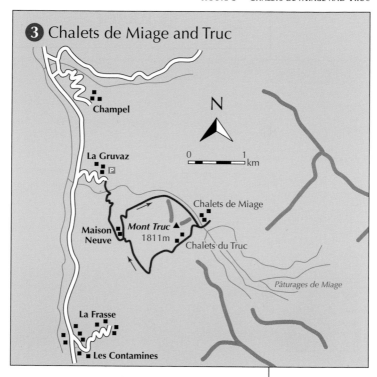

contour around the hillside on a wide track to emerge eventually into the Miage meadows. The path to Le Truc goes straight off to the right, but first go across the river to the **Chalets de Miage** for lunch.

That done, retrace your steps and climb the small and usually quite hot trail, flanked by alder bushes, up to the Truc plateau. The **Chalets du Truc** café is easy to spot, with its picnic tables and awnings. After drinks here pick up the forest track heading south. Quite soon there is a junction where you turn right on an equally wide track. Stay on this and you will eventually arrive at the junction just above Maison Neuve. Retrace your steps to the car park.

# ROUTE 4

*Charousse*

| | |
|---|---|
| **Start/Finish** | Amis de la Nature building 1131m |
| **Distance** | 5km |
| **Time** | 1hr 45min |
| **Terrain** | Easy paths |
| **Altitude gain** | Around 200m |
| **Map** | Top 25 3531 ET Saint-Gervais-les-Bains |
| **Parking** | Les Chavants/La Côte. From the west end of Les Houches drive up to Les Chavants and look for the Amis de la Nature building on the left. There is parking space at the entrance and also just further up the road on the left. |
| **Note** | Dogs allowed |

The hamlet of Charousse is like a film set – picture-perfect old-style rustic chalets set in a beautiful clearing with the most beautiful backdrop of the Mont Blanc massif. It has indeed been used for several films and has acquired a somewhat mythical status – at least in the realm of 'perfect mountain hamlets'.

This easy and short walk takes a circular route around and above the hamlet, coming back through it for the return.

From the road by the Amis de la Nature building, turn left up a trail (signed to Les Granges des Chavants, Col de la Forclaz and Col de Voza), which climbs quite steeply before levelling off at a junction above Charousse. Go straight ahead at this junction then soon fork right on a path that contours just above the hamlet. After around three-quarters of a kilometre, a wide trail heads left up to the Col de la Forclaz – don't take this. Instead, stay right and follow the gently descending path through the forest to a sharp bend back right. Continue on the same trail, which becomes a wide rough track, until you reach a sharp left bend. Here you continue straight ahead and in a short distance you'll cross a stream, after which you

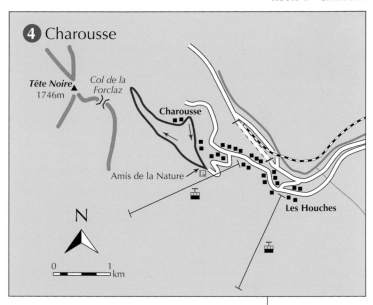

### 4 Charousse

*Tête Noire*
1746m

*Col de la Forclaz*

**Charousse**

Amis de la Nature → P

**Les Houches**

N

0   1
⊢━━━━┥km

need to turn right and briefly climb uphill to reach the bottom corner of **Charousse**. You can now stroll all the

*The indisputable beauty of Charousse*

*The sign says it all*

way across the charming hamlet, enjoying those spectacular views of the massif and beyond. Keep left after the hamlet and go down a wide track through woods to come out on the road above the Ecole de Physique and then along to the Amis de la Nature.

 **ROUTE 5**

*Lac du Brévent*

| | |
|---|---|
| **Start/Finish** | Top of the two-part cable car at the summit of Le Brévent 2525m |
| **Distance** | 3.5km |
| **Time** | 1hr down; 1hr 30min–2hr return |
| **Terrain** | The trail is waymarked and well maintained, but rocky underfoot. |
| **Altitude gain** | About 400m |
| **Map** | Top 25 3531 ET Saint-Gervais-les-Bains |
| **Parking** | The Planpraz/Brévent car park on the top end of Chamonix |
| **Note** | No dogs allowed |

The view of Mont Blanc from the Brévent is really striking, so any walk in this area will allow you to savour those views. Nowadays the two-stage Planpraz/Brévent lift system gets you to the summit in no time and gives access to some lovely walks. Take a good pair of binoculars and enjoy spotting climbers on the slopes of the glaciated peaks opposite.

A good objective for families is the Lac du Brévent – 400m below the summit of the Brévent itself. The fact that the lake is below the starting point is important as that makes this walk the opposite to most alpine hikes – you start the day with a descent and finish with a fairly relentless and often very hot climb back up to the cable car. Allow yourself plenty of time. Leaving the return until the last minute will result in a breathless and sweaty race against the clock, which would rather spoil this beautiful day out.

It was from the top of the Brévent (the mountain, not the cable car) that in the late 18th century **Horace Bénédict de Saussure** first came up with what was

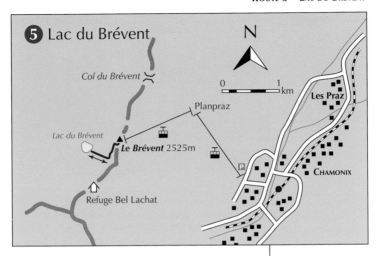

then a radical concept – he wanted to climb to the top of Mont Blanc. Until that time, people did not entertain the notion of climbing glaciated summits – it was regarded as impossible, highly dangerous to attempt and really not desirable either. It took several years for the locals to find a way to the top, motivated not by summit fever but by the large reward offered by de Saussure.

From the lift walk down the wide piste heading south and very soon there is a sign pointing left to the Lac du Brévent and the Refuge Bel Lachat. Take this trail and follow it down. The lake can be seen, dark and glittering quite far below. The trail heads to an attractive flattish area where the path goes to the left over towards a rocky ridge. This is a good place to stop and check out the vista: Mont Blanc dominates on the far side, across the valley, with Mont Maudit and Mont Blanc du Tacul on the left of it. To the north you can see the dark depths of the Diosaz valley and, beyond, the rocky barriers of the Fiz and Anterne. In the distance to the west is the rugged Aravis range.

*Wonderful reflections from the small lake above the Lac de Brévent*

A small lake is passed and in calm conditions this gives beautiful reflections of Mont Blanc. Soon after, the path down to the **Lac du Brévent** is signed off to the right, descending steeply through rocks direct to the shore. Take this path and bag your place lakeside for the day.

Return by the same route. The last lift in the summer from the top of the Brévent goes at around 4.30 or 4.45pm – check this before you start your walk.

 ROUTE 6

*Argentière via the Paradis des Praz*

| | |
|---|---|
| **Start** | Place du Mont Blanc, Chamonix 1037m |
| **Finish** | Argentière 1250m |
| **Distance** | 8.5km |
| **Time** | 2hr 30min, or more if the charms of the Paradis des Praz prove too tempting |
| **Terrain** | The trails are all excellent. |
| **Altitude gain** | About 200m |
| **Map** | Top 25 3630 OT Chamonix Mont Blanc |
| **Parking** | Place du Mont Blanc, Chamonix – underground car park by the roundabout near to the Hotel Alpina. There are also several open-air car parks along the main road heading out of town. |
| **Note** | Dogs allowed |

A very logical route following the Arve River from Chamonix to Argentière, while enjoying beautiful views of the soaring Chamonix Aiguilles and the Drus.

The Paradis des Praz is idyllically situated next to a stream that feeds into the Arve and is indeed a paradise for small children, who will delight in playing by the stream and eating ice creams. There are also donkeys in high season. The route continues past Les Tines and up to Argentière. Nowhere is the trail at all steep but if anyone has had enough they could hop on the train at Les Tines. Otherwise, the train can be used to return from Argentière, or there is also the Chamonix Bus service.

Go into the Place Mont Blanc and take the track out right (north) alongside the **River Arve**, passing a playground on the right. This wide track continues next to the river, past the sports centre, then over the river and crosses several small roads – it is signed to Les Praz. Eventually you'll emerge onto the road coming from Chamonix to Les

*Most houses in the area will be well decorated with flowers in the summer*

93

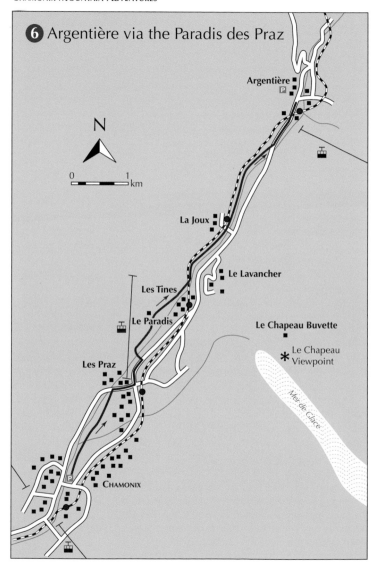

**6** Argentière via the Paradis des Praz

Argentière

La Joux

Le Lavancher

Les Tines

Le Paradis

Le Chapeau Buvette

**∗** Le Chapeau Viewpoint

Les Praz

*Mer de Glace*

CHAMONIX

N

0      1
km

Praz. Take this road briefly as far as the Hotel Labrador and the golf course. Turn into the Hotel Labrador then take a track going off to the right along the other side of the river, signed to the Paradis des Praz. ▶ Soon you'll reach the **Paradis des Praz**, where there is usually a *buvette*, sometimes donkeys and on any hot summer's day there will be people by the water.

Stay on the walking trail. Whatever you do, don't venture onto the golf course!

The wide track continues past a first bridge to a second one at **Les Tines**. Don't go over the river but take the trail right alongside it and continue on this all the way until eventually you reach the main road at the entrance to **Argentière**. Go up the road to find the train station on the right.

# ROUTE 7
## *Le Chapeau*

| | |
|---|---|
| **Start/Finish** | Le Lavancher 1250m |
| **Distance** | 4km |
| **Time** | 2hr 30min |
| **Terrain** | The trail is excellent. |
| **Altitude gain** | 330m |
| **Map** | Top 25 3630 OT Chamonix Mont Blanc |
| **Parking** | At the top of the village of Le Lavancher |
| **Note** | Dogs allowed |

Long before the cable cars were built this was a must-do walk. In those days the Mer de Glace was a rather bigger glacier than it is today, but even in these days of receding ice this walk is a classic. The views from the trail are spectacular well before you reach the viewpoint at Le Chapeau. En route in. the forest tantalising windows through the sparse trees show the whole of the Chamonix valley spread out below, with the Bossons Glacier and the Goûter Ridge of Mont Blanc particularly striking. Once at the viewpoint, the Mer de Glace is seen, now rather far below.

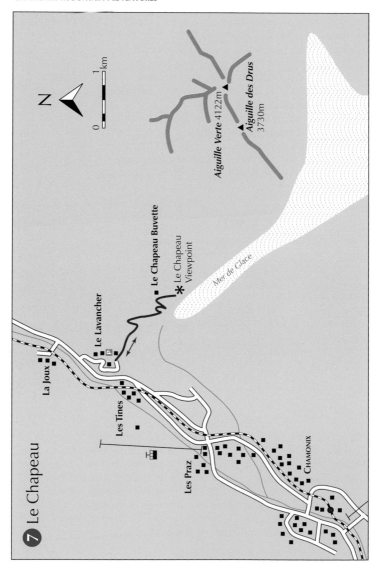

**7** Le Chapeau

Aiguille Verte 4122m

Aiguille des Drus 3730m

Le Chapeau Buvette

* Le Chapeau Viewpoint

Mer de Glace

Le Lavancher

La Joux

Les Tines

Les Praz

CHAMONIX

Two glacial lakes have formed where once the snout of the glacier filled the valley and the sad remnants of this once imposing icy mass are visible. Further up, however, the river of ice is still impressive and the peaks behind are imposing and majestic – the Dent de Géant soars up at the end of the valley. Nearer, the rocky spire of the Drus is particularly imposing, as are the Aiguilles de Chamonix on the other side of the glacier.

From the car park just walk up the road a few minutes to a footpath sign which directs you into the forest for Le Chapeau. All that remains is to follow the signs, and in about 50min you'll reach the café at **Le Chapeau**. The path goes on to the right and after another 15min the **viewpoint** is reached. The café is handy for refreshments before the return to the car park by the same route.

*The viewpoint at Le Chapeau gives a great view of the Mer de Glace and the glacial lakes now forming as the glacier retreats*

**ROUTE 8**

*Montroc–Col des Montets–Vallorcine*

| | |
|---|---|
| **Start** | Montroc 1382m |
| **Finish** | Vallorcine 1260m |
| **Distance** | 6km |
| **Time** | 2hr but this doesn't allow for time spent at the Chalet de la Réserve |
| **Terrain** | The trails are all excellent and well signed. |
| **Altitude gain** | 80m |
| **Map** | Top 25 3630 OT Chamonix Mont Blanc |
| **Parking** | Montroc train station |
| **Note** | Not suitable for dogs because of the short section over the Col des Montets, which is in the Aiguilles Rouges Réserve. |

Another half-day route, but one that is full of interest and a good way to use the train for a linear walk.

This walk will take you via the pretty hamlet of Trè-le-Champ, over the Col des Montets, with the chance to visit the Chalet de la Réserve des Aiguilles Rouges; then it's down a delightful trail into Vallorcine with tea and cakes at the station café before taking the train back to Montroc. The route could even be extended right down to the Swiss frontier, which although not particularly scenic or interesting in itself, does have the attraction of being an international frontier (and how often do you walk from one country to another?), as well as offering several chocolate shops!

The Chalet de la Réserve on the Col des Montets is definitely worth a visit as it houses a good display of stuffed animals commonly found in the Alps and lots of information on the flowers of the area. It sells nature books and postcards, as well as cold drinks, which could be welcome on a hot summer's day.

From Montroc station head towards the railway tunnel and take the trail that goes over the top of it (northwards). Follow the signs to **Trè-le-Champ** – it's prettiest to go all the way through the hamlet, rather than skirting above it, so you can enjoy the flowery gardens and old houses.

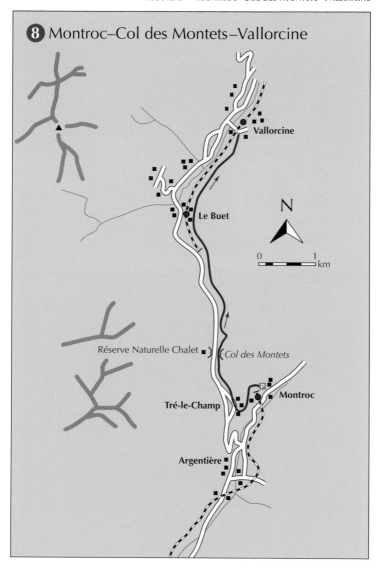

**8** Montroc–Col des Montets–Vallorcine

Vallorcine

Le Buet

N

0   1 km

Réserve Naturelle Chalet ■ ⟩( *Col des Montets*

P
Montroc

Tré-le-Champ ■

Argentière ■

*The Reserve Naturelle chalet at the Col des Montets is definitely worth a visit*

This section is part of the botanical footpath that makes a circuit from the Chalet de la Réserve, and there are signs telling you the names of the plants you'll see on the way.

A wide track leads out of the hamlet both north and south – go north (right) until you reach the main road. A very short section along the road soon brings you to a small footpath just next to the road, rising alongside the forest. This crosses a car park and then becomes a very pleasant open trail up to the **Col de Montets** (1461m). ◀

Once at the pass, stay on the right-hand side of the road. There is a side road that heads off from the car park and avoids walking on the main road. At the end of this, walk a few metres next to the main road then take a small trail right to join a wide track that goes down the broad valley before continuing next to a stream. A small path heads out over a little bridge to the road near **Le Buet**, but ignore this and stay on the trail straight ahead, which rises slightly before continuing in the trees, going past a small house on the left. Le Buet train station is seen on the left, surrounded by chalets. The trail continues past some more houses down through meadows. The railway line is parallel to the trail now, on the left. Keep it on the left and go straight on, down a slope to the flat meadows and football field to **Vallorcine**, arriving at the level crossing.

There is a café at the station and trains run hourly (more or less) back to Montroc (and Chamonix).

### 🚶 ROUTE 9
*Bérard valley and Sur le Rocher*

| | |
|---|---|
| **Start/Finish** | Le Buet 1350m |
| **Distance** | 3.5km |
| **Time** | 2hr–2hr 30 min (could be done more quickly but it's worth taking the time to enjoy the scenery) |
| **Terrain** | The trails are all excellent. |
| **Altitude gain** | 200m |
| **Map** | Top 25 3630 OT Chamonix Mont Blanc |
| **Parking** | Le Buet, opposite the Hôtel du Buet |
| **Note** | The Bérard valley forms its own reserve and a sign at the entrance says dogs are not allowed. However, at Vallorcine Tourist Office they say they are allowed on a lead. |

The Bérard valley is one of the gems of Vallorcine: a beautiful river runs down from the high peaks at the head of the corrie, culminating in a vertical waterfall just before the water runs out to join the somewhat sadly named Eau Noire in the main valley. Alongside this clear flowing river there is a much-travelled trail, which leads all the way up to the Refuge Pierre à Bérard.

On this walk we just venture into the Bérard valley, past the waterfall and onwards a little way, past some excellent paddling spots, to then break out and saunter up to the tiny hamlet of Sur le Rocher where the views across the valley are superb.

A steep trail leads down from the houses to re-join the Vallorcine valley, making this a lovely half-day ramble.

From **Le Buet** take the signed trail uphill from the hotel and go past the old houses at La Poya. The way onwards

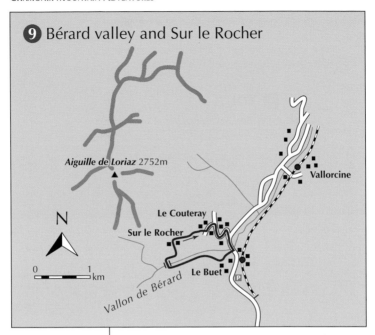

## ➒ Bérard valley and Sur le Rocher

**Aiguille de Loriaz** 2752m

**Vallorcine**

N

0        1
▬▬▬km

**Le Couteray**

**Sur le Rocher**

**Le Buet**

P

*Vallon de Bérard*

From here you can see vestiges of what must have been a very precarious walkway used in times past.

through the sparse larch forest is clearly signed to the Cascade de Bérard. Once there you can visit the café (renowned for its *tarte aux myrtilles*), and from the wide terrace you can look down at the waterfall. ◄ There is a relatively recent metal walkway that leads round to look at the waterfall. Very good, impressive views and accessible to all except dogs, which might not like the lattice work metal structure.

On Thursdays in high season the local Guides offer a rope traverse (a 'Tyrolien') across the void.

An information sign tells about the nearby **Grotte de Farinet**, a cave where it is claimed a chap called Farinet hung out in the mid 19th century. Farinet is said to have made counterfeit money and

*The Bérard River is clear – and very cold*

distributed it locally, which would explain why the locals were happy for him to hideout in their cave!

Getting back to our walk, leave the café and go back across the little bridge. Head up the valley, enjoying the pretty stream, until you reach another bridge – with a sign that says 'Font Froide'. This is where you leave the Bérard, so go across the bridge and pick up the trail that goes back along the other side of the valley, rising gently to arrive on a flatter area among forest. A short continuation of the trail brings you out at the small houses of **Sur le Rocher**. Go through the houses on the right to get great views across to the Aiguille Verte, among other peaks. This is a good place to break before embarking on the steep but well-maintained trail down (eastwards) from the houses, which pops out at **Le Couteray**. From there, it's a short walk down the road to the main road, then turn right to get back to Le Buet.

 **ROUTE 10**

*Dinosaur tracks*

| | |
|---|---|
| **Start/Finish** | Emosson 1960m |
| **Distance** | 8.5km (more if you don't use the shuttle bus outward to cross the dam) |
| **Time** | 5–6hr |
| **Terrain** | The trails are generally good and well signed but the descent of the Veudale Gorge is rocky and quite steep. Better to go out and back along the outward trail if there is anyone in the group who is very small or not used to walking on rough ground. As noted above, do not go until the snow has melted on north-facing slopes. Don't underestimate the time needed to descend the gorge – if in doubt return by the outward trail. |
| **Altitude gain** | 550m |
| **Map** | Top 25 3630 OT Chamonix Mont Blanc |
| **Parking** | Emosson dam |
| **Note** | Dogs allowed |

This walk, like the Lacs Jovet walk (Family Walks, Route 2), is longer than the others described as Family Walks, but it deserves to be in this section because going to see real dinosaur tracks is a unique experience. It is suitable for families used to hiking in the mountains.

It's not every day you go out and see footprints left by now extinct creatures that roamed the earth hundreds of millions of years ago, and the tracks up above the Emosson Lakes are definitely worth visiting as they are clearly defined and quite numerous. But don't wait too long: take your kids now because if you wait until they've got kids it might be too late – these tracks, made in the Triassic era 250 millions years ago, are most likely going to disappear in the next half century due to erosion.

The area around Vieux Emosson and Emosson Lake is in upheaval for a while, due to the pump storage construction (see box 'The Emosson Lakes Region' in the introduction). However, it's worth doing battle with the trucks and construction mess because once you're past the Vieux Emosson dam the cirque is really beautiful and the tracks are well worth the visit.

This walk can be done as a there and back via the small road from the Emosson Lake. However, the return down the Veudale gorge is much nicer, so that's the way described here, but it is longer and rougher underfoot.

It's important to note that this is not a walk for early summer. The tracks are on a north-facing slope at 2400m so they remain under snow until well into the summer. Also the descent of the Veudale Gorge should only be undertaken when it is snow-free.

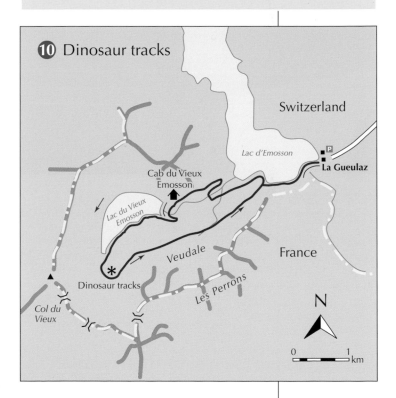

It is a testament to the relative remoteness of the Vieux Emosson cirque that these very well-preserved **footprints** and wave ripple marks were not

*The beautiful Emosson
lake and dam*

discovered until 1976, by a French geologist who luckily was well enough informed to know what he was looking at. The tracks were made by quite small dinosaurs – at least their hands and feet must have been small. However, it's fairly mind blowing to see these and to imagine that they were made before the mountains even existed, when this was all ocean. Casts have been made of the prints and are now stored for posterity at a museum in Geneva, but seeing those there won't be anything like seeing the real thing.

Walk down the small road beyond the restaurant, or go directly onto the road behind the dinosaur. This small road takes you to the huge dam, which you walk across. Information boards provide some interesting facts as you cross. Keep going on the road around the lake to reach the junction with the steep road up to Vieux Emosson.

Once at the bottom of the small road walk up it past the **Cabane du Vieux Emosson**, which is a café and a mountain hut.

Go through a tunnel and then follow a good path around the south side of the **Vieux Emosson Lake**. At the end of the lake the path rises in zigzags to eventually go across left (south) to the dinosaur tracks, which are protected by chain barriers. ▶

There is an information board and sometimes during the summer there is a geologist on hand to give extra details.

When you've finished looking at the tracks, to reach the head of the Veudale gorge you have to climb a short but steep slope found by continuing along the trail past the footprints heading north-east. The climb is not too long but is quite arduous. Once at the top a nice flat section feels like you're on top of the world, above the lake. The head of the **Veudale** gorge is quickly attained and the way down the gorge is fairly obvious. However, take care because there are loose stones on the trail and it is pretty steep at the start. After a few zigzags the slope starts to ease off and the barren rocky ground gives way to grassy terrain, and a very pretty descent. ▶

Look out for marmots as they are often to be seen scurrying from burrow to burrow, or lazing on rocky ledges.

The route gets easier and easier but goes on rather longer than expected. Finally, just as the legs are getting tired, you'll exit onto the road, leading all the way across the dam and back to the car park.

*Small dinosaur tracks made millions of years ago*

# HUT WALKS

 **ROUTE 1**

*Refuge de Platé*

| | |
|---|---|
| **Start/Finish** | Just after Praz Coutant 1171m |
| **Distance** | Roughly 8–9km |
| **Time** | 2hr 30min to the hut; 1hr 30min down |
| **Terrain** | The main part of the walk ascends a very steep and usually very hot gully, but the path is well maintained with lots of zigzags. |
| **Altitude gain** | 861m |
| **Map** | IGN Top 25 3530 ET Samoëns |
| **Parking** | Car park on the right on the road between the Plateau d'Assy and Plaine Joux, just after Praz Coutant and just before the Residence Le Fonteney |
| **Hut details** | Altitude 2032m; no showers; dormitories; tel 04 50 93 11 07 |

The Refuge de Platé is an old summer farm building where in times past the locals would bring their animals to graze for the high summer season. Since then it was used during World War II by the resistance (*Maquis*) and after that was bought by the Club Alpin Français. It is a beautiful place to spend a night in the mountains, surrounded by meadows and limestone peaks, far above the Arve valley.

The views encompass the Mont Blanc massif (of course), Mont Joly and, just beyond, the Aravis chain.

The route is described from the Plateau d'Assy, but a shorter approach is from the top of the Grandes Platières cable car at Flaine, from where a 1hr downhill walk across the limestone plateau brings you to the hut rather less out of breath than the way described here. However, Plateau d'Assy is a shorter drive from Chamonix and that cold beer will be far more deserved hiking up this way.

A small road leaves the road by the Residence Le Fonteney and is signed to the Refuge de Platé. Follow the undulating wide track north-west which goes around

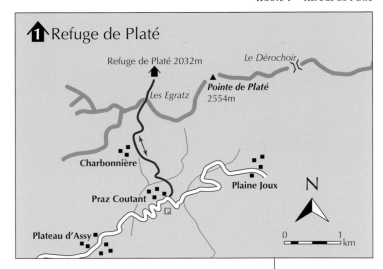

# Refuge de Platé

Refuge de Platé 2032m

Le Dérochoir

Les Egratz

▲ **Pointe de Platé**
2554m

**Charbonnière**

**Plaine Joux**

**Praz Coutant**

N

**Plateau d'Assy**

0     1
⬛⬛⬛⬛ km

to **Charbonnière**. You'll find a trail heading off right, up **Les Egratz**. Crane your neck and you'll see it goes a long way up and very steeply. Gird your loins and set off. It's worth it once you reach the top! Once up there take time

*The Refuge de Platé – you'll need a cold beer after making the climb up here*

to catch your breath and enjoy the views before strolling over grassy meadows to the hut and a well-deserved beer!

Return by the same route.

 **ROUTE 2**

*Refuge de Tré-la-Tête*

| | |
|---|---|
| **Start/Finish** | Cugnon, just south of Les Contamines-Montjoie, 1200m |
| **Distance** | 6.25km |
| **Time** | 2hr to the hut; 1hr 30min down |
| **Terrain** | Good trail in the forest |
| **Altitude gain** | 770m |
| **Map** | IGN Top 25 3531 ET Saint-Gervais-les-Bains |
| **Parking** | Car park at the end of the road in Cugnon |
| **Hut details** | Altitude 1970m; showers; rooms and dormitories; tel 04 50 47 01 68 |

The Tré-la-Tête Hut (marked as Hôtel de Tré-la-Tête on the map) is in a commanding position way above the Contamines-Montjoie valley. It is reached by a beautiful shady trail through forest, alongside wild raspberry bushes and mountain ash, and as you climb the views appear, with the impressive Mont Joly ridge in the foreground.

This is a fine hut to go to for an overnight as the accommodation is old-style mountain inn, with rooms available, great food and, most important of all, a warm welcome. It's worth taking the time to walk on above the hut to view the terminal snout of the Tré-la-Tête Glacier.

From the car park take the trail signed to Tré-la-Tête, which goes above the hamlet. The trail goes up to join another coming from Les Loyers, then higher up take the right-hand junction twice, leaving the path to Armancette on the left. You'll go under the climbing cliff of Les Plans to emerge from the forest at an area of bushes. A trail goes off right to Le Praz, but continue straight on to another junction where there is a choice for Tré-la-Tête – the option on the right

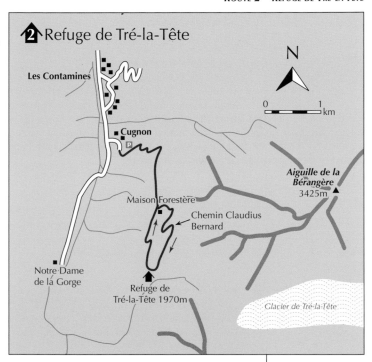

**2** Refuge de Tré-la-Tête

N

0    1 km

**Les Contamines**

**Cugnon**
P

Maison Forestère

Chemin Claudius
Bernard

**Aiguille de la
Bérangère**
3425m

Notre Dame
de la Gorge

Refuge de
Tré-la-Tête 1970m

*Glacier de Tré-la-Tête*

*Once a mountain
hotel, the Tré-la-Tête
Hut has maintained
its old traditional
atmosphere high
up above the
Contamines valley*

goes to the hut via the forest, but take the left-hand variant, which is the **Chemin Claudius Bernard**. After a series of zigzags you'll spot the hut, which is quickly reached after a few more bends and a traverse.

To view the glacier, take the trail behind the hut for about 15min.

For the return, either retrace your steps or, for a small variation, take the path which descends to the left of the hut, signed to Cugnon. Switchbacks then a long traverse to the north, below the **Maison Forestière** building, bring you back to the ascent route.

 **ROUTE 3**

*Refuge Moëde d'Anterne*

| | |
|---|---|
| **Start** | Top of the two-part cable car at the summit of Le Brévent 2525m |
| **Finish** | Plaine Joux 1337m |
| **Distance** | 7.5km to the hut; 15.5km in total |
| **Time** | 4hr to the hut; 2hr down |
| **Terrain** | Rocky and slightly technical trail to begin with, getting easier from the Col du Brévent. Tends to hold névé early in the season. |
| **Altitude gain** | 600m |
| **Map** | IGN Top 25 3530 ET Samoëns |
| **Parking** | Planpraz/Brévent car park in Chamonix |
| **Hut details** | Altitude 1996m; showers; rooms and dormitories; tel 04 50 93 60 43 |
| **Note** | The Refuge Moëde d'Anterne is also known as Refuge Chalet Moëde d'Anterne or Refuge du Col d'Anterne |

There has been a hut at Moëde d'Anterne for many years, but the current one was restored in the last 20 years. The result is a large smart building, with good accommodation and facilities, and a super view of the Mont Blanc massif – in short, a great hut to visit. However, be aware this is a really popular hut with visiting hikers and locals alike. The hut can be accessed on

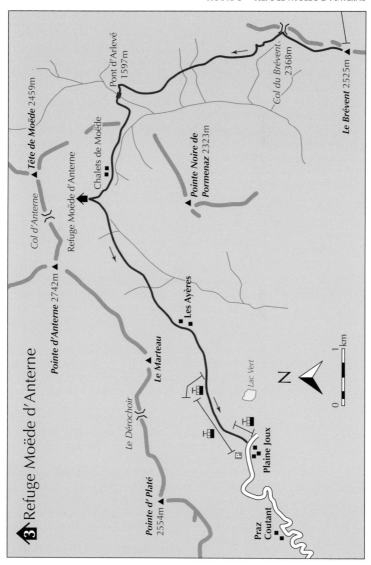

**3** Refuge Moëde d'Anterne

foot either from the Brévent lift or from Plaine Joux, near the Plateau d'Assy (described as the descent here). There also is access for 4x4 vehicles and certain summer weekends can see a lot of traffic. If you feel this could spoil your mountain experience it would be best to avoid such times and go to this hut mid-week.

The route described here is probably best done with an overnight at the hut. The approach is from the top of the Brévent cable car, which gives a wonderful, fairly long hut walk, beginning with a descent to the Pont d'Arlevé then a steady ascent to the hut. This route could be reversed for the return but going out to Plaine Joux gives a less arduous option – the downside being you'll need to pick up the local bus and then the train to get back to Chamonix.

From the top of the cable car take the wide track that leads down and around the hillside. After 5–10min you can't miss a big cairn on the left and a signpost to the Col du Brévent. Go left on this trail, which winds in and out of rocks and boulders, with the occasional cabled section and an easy ladder. This route is interesting and varied but not much fun in rain, when it would be slippery, or in thick fog, when you could just about miss the waymarks, which would be very dangerous.

Once at the **Col du Brévent** the trail onwards down into the valley is fairly obvious. You leave the views of the Mont Blanc massif behind you and instead will have the impressive Diosaz valley below and the Fiz and Anterne cliffs ahead.

The trail makes its way gently down into grassland, past some ruins and onwards until it gets to the **Pont d'Arlevé** (1596m) – often a very warm spot in mid-summer, surrounded by vegetation.

Loins must be girded here as the path ascends through bushy slopes into the higher meadows. You'll see buildings up ahead but this first hamlet just consists of some farm buildings, and you need to continue to reach the hut, which is about on the limit of meadow and barren hillside.

For the return, the easiest option physically, but the more complicated logistically, is to take the jeep track that goes from behind the hut diagonally south-west across the hillside to the attractive chalets of **Les Ayères**, where you'll enjoy one of the most picturesque views of the Mont Blanc massif that exists. From here tracks lead down to **Plaine Joux**. There is a bus service to Le Fayet train station, where you can catch the train back to Chamonix.

*At the Col du Brévent*

# ROUTE 4
*Refuge Bel Lachat*

| | |
|---|---|
| **Start** | Top of the two-part cable car at the summit of Le Brévent 2525m |
| **Finish** | The Planpraz/Brévent car park 1087m |
| **Distance** | 2.5km to the hut; 4.5km hut to Chamonix |
| **Time** | 1hr to the hut; 2hr 30min down to Chamonix. |
| **Terrain** | Well-signed and maintained trail, a tiny bit airy on the ridge before the hut. |
| **Altitude gain** | A few metres of undulation |
| **Map** | IGN Top 25 3531 ET Saint-Gervais-les-Bains |
| **Parking** | Planpraz/Brévent car park in Chamonix |
| **Hut details** | Altitude 2136m; no showers; dormitories; tel 04 50 53 43 23 |

The Refuge Bel Lachat is absolutely one of my favourite huts in the Chamonix valley. It's a basic little wooden shack really, with a living area, a small kitchen you're not encouraged to enter, a double dormitory upstairs and an outside 'Turkish' toilet that flushes over your feet if you're not careful. So, in these days of luxurious mountain refuges it doesn't have a lot going for it – or does it? Perched right on the edge of steep slopes that drop down to the valley, the hut enjoys an indescribably fabulous view of Mont Blanc, not to mention the Chamonix Aiguilles, the Aiguille Verte and the Aravis. The other great attraction is the superbly warm reception from the *gardienne*. Now clearly she won't be there for ever – in 2012 she's already past retirement age – but, whoever is in charge, the hut will still be a real traditional middle mountain hut, and if you get the right weather you'll forever treasure those memories of watching the sunset from the terrace while sipping a glass of (rather rough) red.

From the top of the cable car walk out onto the obvious big track and you'll be able to see your route to the southwest. You can see some grassy summits beyond a big dip with a lake glistening in it. To the left of these peaks you'll see an obvious track going along the edge of the hillside and this is your route. The hut is just out of sight over the edge of this ridge.

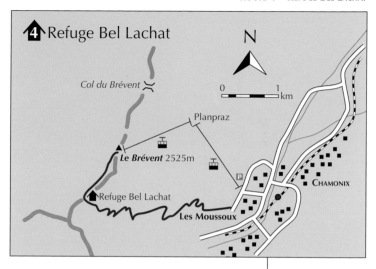

Head down the big track and soon find a signpost off to the left. This leads down a nice wide and rocky trail into the basin below and past a small lake – perfect for reflections. Go around this lake and continue, not being tempted by the diversion right to the bigger lake below – the Lac du Brévent. The trail wanders through rocks then abruptly turns a ridge with some railings and continues along the edge of the main ridge. Follow it along and you'll finally spot the **Refuge Bel Lachat** below. Don't be tempted to go direct – stay on the trail and follow the signs and you'll reach it by a flight of steps.

To return, you could retrace your steps but be sure to allow time to get back up that final slope – harder than you expect after lunch on a sunny afternoon. You do *not* want to miss the last lift down, which is around 5pm, depending on the month.

Better, if you've got the knees for it, is to take the well-signed trail all the way down to Chamonix. It's fairly relentless but the path is well maintained and there's a good chance of seeing ibex en route. And of course all the while you've got those wonderful views of Mont

*On the ridge en route to Bel Lachat, looking across to Mont Blanc*

Blanc and the Chamonix valley to distract you from the grind. You'll pop out at **Les Moussoux** – turn left and in a few minutes you'll be back at the Brévent car park.

 ## ROUTE 5

*Refuge du Lac Blanc*

| | |
|---|---|
| **Start/Finish** | Top of La Flégère cable car 1871m |
| **Distance** | 6km |
| **Time** | 1hr 30min to the hut; 1hr back down |
| **Terrain** | A well-maintained rocky trail but beware – the final part holds névé early in the season. |
| **Altitude gain** | 481m |
| **Map** | IGN Top 25 3630 OT Chamonix Mont Blanc |
| **Parking** | La Flégère cable car station, Les Praz |
| **Hut details** | Altitude 2352m; showers; small dormitories; tel 04 50 53 49 14 |
| **Note** | Refuge du Lac Blanc is also known as Chalet du Lac Blanc |

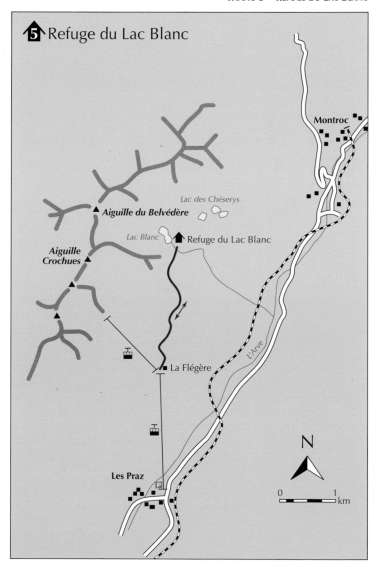

**5** Refuge du Lac Blanc

Montroc

Lac des Chéserys

▲ *Aiguille du Belvédère*

*Lac Blanc*  ▲ Refuge du Lac Blanc

*Aiguille Crochues* ▲

▲

L'Arve

La Flégère

N

Les Praz

0    1 km

It goes without saying that this hut is situated right next to a lake. Lac Blanc is an old glaciated lake and will often be snowy until well into July. It's a beautiful place to visit and this is probably the best-known hut walk in the Chamonix valley, especially since access is made much easier by taking the Flégère cable car. Most people just go for lunch then come back; consequently, midday in high season at Lac Blanc tends to be far from calm, so if you can stay the night this is highly recommended. The hut has excellent facilities and the food is equally good. You'll be able to sit out on the terrace knowing all the crowds are back down in the valley while you watch the sun set on the steep rocky spire of the Drus right opposite.

*Perfect summer conditions at Lac Blanc*

From the top of the cable car the hut route is signed. The trail heads down to a flat place where there is a reservoir then wends its way in a rising traverse across the hillside. It's a really pretty path, with several lovely grassy areas that beg you to sit down and gaze at the view. From Flégère they say you can see 14 glaciers so it's worth taking a break to count them. There's a small lake en route

but it can be dry. Then the trail steepens and well-graded zigzags lead up to the hut.

The return is by the same route, but if you're just having lunch keep an eye on your watch so as to not miss the last lift – around 5.00–5.30pm in mid-summer – and there will probably be a queue. Other alternatives exist but are all more complicated.

# ROUTE 6
*Refuge Albert Premier*

| | |
|---|---|
| **Start** | Top of Le Tour (Balme) chairlift 2100m |
| **Finish** | Le Tour car park 1450m |
| **Distance** | 8.5km |
| **Time** | 2hr to the hut; 1hr 30min down the same route |
| **Terrain** | Good paths all the way. Early in the season there could be névé but the trail isn't steep and the popularity of this hut ensures there will almost always be a good track over any remaining snow. |
| **Altitude gain** | 602m |
| **Map** | IGN Top 25 3630 OT Chamonix Mont Blanc |
| **Parking** | Le Tour cable car |
| **Hut details** | Altitude 2702m; no showers; dormitories; tel 04 50 54 06 20 |

The Albert Premier Hut is perched above the Tour Glacier, towards the head of the Chamonix valley. Named after King Albert of Belgium, a keen alpinist who died in the mountains, this refuge is used to access the Aiguilles du Tour summit, one of the best moderate peaks of the area. So, you've guessed it – it gets very, very busy. Guides flock there with their clients and most nights during the summer season the hut is bursting at the seams. Unless you enjoy trying to sleep crammed in with lots of other sweaty bodies, this is not the place to go for that magical night in the mountains.

However, it's a great objective for lunch and will give a good walk with wonderful glacier scenery.

From the top of the chairlift take the very obvious trail heading around the hillside southwards to the often

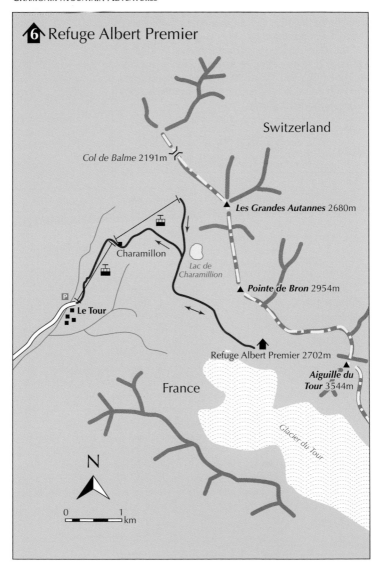

**6** Refuge Albert Premier

Switzerland

Col de Balme 2191m

▲ *Les Grandes Autannes* 2680m

Charamillon

*Lac de Charamillion*

▲ *Pointe de Bron* 2954m

P

■ **Le Tour**

Refuge Albert Premier 2702m

▲ *Aiguille du Tour* 3544m

France

*Glacier du Tour*

N

0        1 km

dried-up **Lac de Charamillon**. The path continues, rising gradually to turn the ridge and giving great views of the glacier and the Aiguille du Chardonnet.

After a short section of rocky ground the good trail resumes and the hut can be seen on the hillside well above the glacier, and is soon reached along a maintained section of moraine trail.

For the descent, it's best to take the same route in reverse, at least as far as a junction just before the Lac de Charamillon. Here you could go left and avoid taking the chairlift down. You'll arrive at the café at **Charamillon** at the top of the cable car and you could take this down or follow the well-signed path, under the lift, back to Le Tour.

*The Tour Glacier with the Albert Premier Hut at the end of the moraine ridge on the left*

**ROUTE 7**

*Refuge de la Pierre à Bérard*

| | |
|---|---|
| **Start/Finish** | Hôtel du Buet 1350m |
| **Distance** | 10km |
| **Time** | 2hr to the hut: 1hr back down (more if distracted by paddling opportunities en route) |
| **Terrain** | Easy and well-maintained trail all the way |
| **Altitude gain** | 575m |
| **Map** | IGN Top 25 3630 OT Chamonix Mont Blanc |
| **Parking** | Le Buet |
| **Hut details** | Altitude 1925m; no showers; dormitories; tel 04 50 54 62 08 |

The tiny Pierre à Bérard Hut is nestled under its rock several kilometres up the beautiful and wild Bérard valley. In summer the hut seems always to be busy, bustling from lunchtime until late afternoon with thirsty hikers, who've either come up for the day or who are descending from Mont Buet. In winter, however, you'd struggle even to see the hut as it is buried under several metres of snow, which drifts up around the big boulder the hut is built under.

The Bérard valley can be described as 'wild' even though it is incredibly popular on warm summer days. From the inviting buvette above the Bérard Cascade at the bottom of the valley all the way along the babbling Bérard river, people will be picnicking, paddling, sunbathing … some won't get beyond the first inviting pools by the waterfall, others will hike up to the higher flat area where the views open up.

Despite this, the valley has a feeling of grandeur, formed by rocky crags and grassy slopes. Mont Buet looms far above, and is a much sought-after goal for walkers, as at 3096m it is the highest peak in the Aiguilles Rouges.

From **Le Buet** a trail starts just up from the hotel and is signed to the Cascade du Bérard. Take this trail and go through the old buildings of La Poya, where the first people settled in the Vallorcine valley, several hundred years

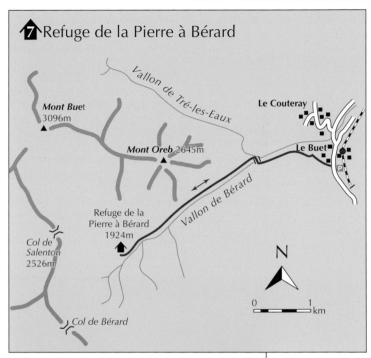

**7** Refuge de la Pierre à Bérard

Vallon de Tré-les-Eaux

**Mont Buet**
3096m

**Mont Oreb** 2645m

Le Couteray

Le Buet

P

Vallon de Bérard

Refuge de la
Pierre à Bérard
1924m

*Col de
Salenton*
2526m

*Col de Bérard*

N

0          1 km

*The Aiguilles Rouges
seen from above
the Refuge Pierre à
Bérard, early morning
after bad weather*

ago. The trail is easy to follow and it goes around and into the **Bérard Valley** just next to the Cascade de Bérard and the *buvette*, where it's worth a stop for the renowned *tarte aux myrtilles*.

Continue up the valley and cross the next bridge to the other side of the river to take the trail alongside the true left bank of the river. The valley becomes quite enclosed but, after a steepening, the path emerges from the forest to the flatter upper Bérard valley, which is at the limit of the treeline and thus more open and brighter. With good eyesight you'll spot the hut nestling under the slopes higher up. The route is obvious and is relatively gentle until the final push to the hut.

Return by the same route.

# ROUTE 8

*Refuge de Loriaz*

| | |
|---|---|
| **Start/Finish** | Le Couteray in the Vallorcine valley 1360m |
| **Distance** | 7.5km |
| **Time** | 1hr 45min to the hut; 1hr back down |
| **Terrain** | Easy rising path all the way |
| **Altitude gain** | 660m |
| **Map** | IGN Top 25 3630 OT Chamonix Mont Blanc |
| **Parking** | Le Couteray |
| **Hut details** | Altitude 2020m; no showers; dormitories; tel 04 50 54 06 45 |

The Loriaz alpage (summer grazing meadows) belongs to the village of Vallorcine and has been used by local farmers for centuries for grazing in the height of the summer. Nowadays the main farm building at Loriaz is used as a summer hut, with several outbuildings for dormitories and facilities, but the cows are still present. The hut provides traditional food and accommodation and, being at 2000m and well above the treeline, it enjoys uninterrupted views of the Mont Blanc massif, notably Mont Blanc itself and the Aiguilles Verte, Chardonnet and Tour.

The buildings face east, so breakfast can be enjoyed outside in the summer – what better way to start the day!

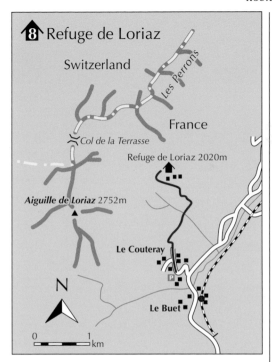

Walk out of **Le Couteray** on a wide track, signposted to Loriaz. This track winds up past some houses, then after a sharp bend left there is a footpath heading up into the forest on the right. Take this and continue past a junction where you don't go right, and after several zigzags you'll pop out onto the wide track again. Turn right and go up to the next bend. Here a footpath continues straight ahead and is again signed to Loriaz. Take this and just keep going – it goes gently at first, over a gushing stream, and then begins to steepen, ascending in several zigzags until it emerges from the forest.

Views of the Mont Blanc massif now open up and it won't be long before you're ascending the final grassy meadows to reach the hut. The hut itself isn't seen until

127

*The delightful alpage of Loriaz*

the last minute – a line of triangular roofs will appear just as you're starting to question where it is.

The simplest return is by the same route.

**Transhumance** is the farming process whereby the cattle are taken to higher and higher meadows as the summer progresses, in search of the best and freshest grass. In early September the animals are brought back down to the valley after what has hopefully been a successful season with the production of lots of cheese for the winter months.

# ADVENTURE WALKS

 **ROUTE 1**

*Pointe Percée*

| | |
|---|---|
| **Start/Finish** | Burzier 904m |
| **Distance** | 15km |
| **Time** | 10hr |
| **Terrain** | Steep footpaths followed by rocky scrambling |
| **High point** | Pointe Percée 2750m |
| **Altitude gain** | 1846m |
| **Map** | Top 25 3530 OT Cluses Sallanches |
| **Parking** | Burzier |

The Pointe Percée is the highest point of the spectacular limestone range of the Aravis and owes its name to the hole on its north ridge. It also has a characteristic finger of rock (Le Doigt). From its summit at 2750m, you feel like you could reach across the lower Arve valley and touch Mont Blanc. There are no really easy routes to the top of this mountain. Both its *voies normales* are on the sporty side. The route described here, 'les cheminées de Sallanches', is the harder of the two – but only by a whisker. You'll need to feel comfortable on quite exposed scrambly terrain and probably be equipped with a rope if you have a nervous friend. Make sure the forecast is good – a rainstorm could be a real headache.

Keep a lookout skywards while walking here (obviously not on the rocky sections where your eyes should be on your feet!). For the past 25 years the Aravis has been the scene of the reintroduction programme for the Bearded Vulture (*Gypaete Barbu*). These huge and graceful birds have a wingspan not far off 3m and a striking orange underbelly, and only flap about once an hour. Seeing one of these fly overhead is one of the unexpected joys of walking in the Aravis.

From the car park at **Burzier**, follow the 4x4 track up to the alpage at **Doran**. (It is possible to drive up the first part of this track with a normal car to a higher parking place at the junction with the Mayères track.) There is a

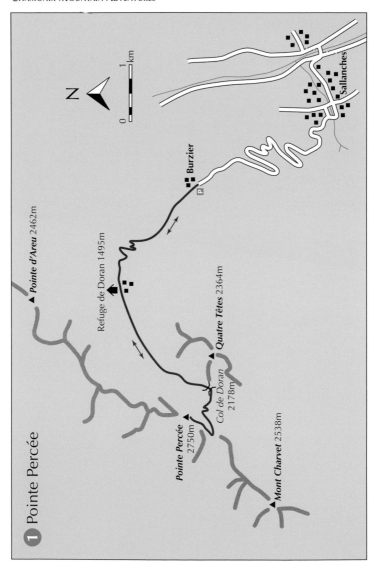

Pointe Percée

*Heading back down to the Col de Doran*

pleasant traditional refuge at Doran, where it's possible to stay, and given the length of this hike this option is desirable. ▶ The finger of rock on the side of the Pointe Percée summit is very obvious from here.

From the hut take the footpath leading initially up the beautiful green Doran valley. Higher up, the grass gives way to shale and the slopes steepen until, after a few steep zigzags, you emerge on the **Col de Doran** (2178m). From here an indistinct path strikes right, up very steep slopes to the Col des Vert – it is actually much easier than it looks! Once on the col, start looking for yellow paint marks, which head into the white limestone ramparts of the mountain. Delightful scrambling following these yellow marks leads via a final steep 'pitch' onto the narrow ridge. (There is a large steel piton at the top of this pitch to protect the rest of your party and also provide an anchor for the descent.) Now scramble along the ridge past the exit of the other normal route, which comes up a wide rocky couloir from the left (this route is marked

A nearby farm offers local cheese for sale and is worth a visit.

131

*The moon guards the summit of the Pointe Percée*

with red paint flashes). Carry on winding up the ridge to the summit of **Pointe Percée** (2750m), which is equipped with a cross and a summit book.

Descend by the same route.

 **ROUTE 2**

*The Dérochoir and Désert de Platé*

| | |
|---|---|
| **Start/Finish** | Plaine Joux 1337m |
| **Distance** | 11.7km |
| **Time** | 6hr 30min |
| **Terrain** | These are reasonably good mountain paths, though the aided section to the Dérochoir is quite long. The descent is relentless but the trail is well made. This route requires the paths to be snow-free – névé lingers a long time on the northern slopes of the Pointe de Platé. |
| **High point** | Col de la Portette 2354m |
| **Altitude gain** | 1020m |
| **Map** | Top 25 3530 ET Samoëns |
| **Parking** | Plaine Joux |

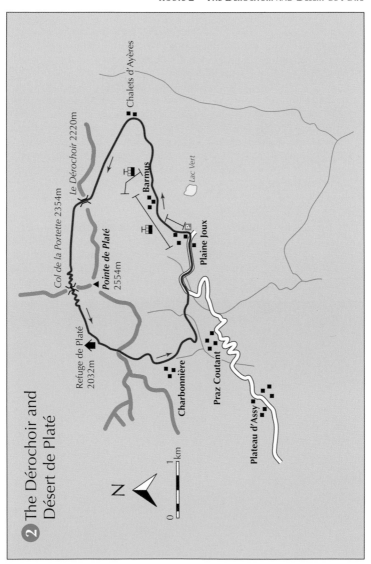

**2** The Dérochoir and Désert de Platé

Chalets d'Ayères

Le Dérochoir 2220m

Col de la Portette 2354m

Barmus

Lac Vert

Pointe de Platé 2554m

Plaine Joux

Refuge de Platé 2032m

Charbonnière

Praz Coutant

Plateau d'Assy

N

0 — 1 km

Seen from the Arve valley, the Rochers de Fiz present an apparently impenetrable barrier. The Dérochoir is the only obvious break in the cliff and it's graphically named, from the verb *dérocher* meaning to scour or clear of rocks. The Dérochoir is a landslide channel forming the only weakness in the cliffs and it's through this that our path makes its way up and onto the wonderful limestone plateau of the Désert de Platé, a paradoxical haven of barren rock and flowery meadows situated high above the valley.

The way through the Dérochoir requires the aid of cables and ladders but gives a spectacular adventure walk set against the background of the Mont Blanc massif and the Aravis peaks. After the excitement of the ladders, a nice trail leads to the Refuge de Platé before a steep descent to complete this spectacular circuit.

*The Dérochoir seen from Ayères*

Starting from the **Plaine Joux** car park it's not immediately obvious where the footpath goes as there are several false tracks which are ski pistes. Head around right to the cafés and a sign indicates all paths up and left. Go up the track that goes to **Ayères**. There are several clusters of chalets,

all called Ayères and the path goes through Ayères des Rocs and Ayères des Pierrières. Just after the chalets look out for a path going left to the Dérochoir, which is way-marked in red and rises gently at first. The sign in French and English warns that the path is dangerous, because of the rocks and the cabled section.

Boulder-fields have to be crossed before you reach the meat of the trail, the chains and ladders. This is the fun part and after it's done only a short walk is needed to reach the **Dérochoir** (2220m). Behind, the Mont Blanc massif presents its full glory while ahead a whole new vista opens up: the limestone pavement of Platé with its characteristic crevasses and huge waves of grey rock. Beyond, the rock gives way to grassy meadows where the Chalets de Sales enjoy an idyllic position.

The **Col de la Portette** (2354m) can be seen apparently not too far away to the left (west). It's wise not to linger as this pass is further than it looks, partly because the rocky ground makes for slow progress. Once at the col you can see the **Refuge de Platé**, which is your next objective, but your gaze will be drawn to the Arve valley spread out thousands of metres below. Beyond is Mont Joly and still further away the Aravis range.

Take the opportunity for a cold drink at the hut before girding your loins, or at least your knees, for the impending descent. This is preceded by a delightful wander across grassy meadows to the edge where the world drops away and the horror of the descent path is revealed – zigzags as far as the eye can see! Take a deep breath and just get on with it – it will end – sooner or later. Once down at the treeline breathe a sigh of relief as you finish on the flat track, following it leftwards to an easy-to-miss path on the left signed 'Plaine Joux 20 mins'. This comes out onto the road 10min away from Plaine Joux.

**ROUTE 3**

*Aiguille du Belvédère*

| | |
|---|---|
| **Start** | Top of the Index chairlift 2385m |
| **Finish** | Top of La Flégère cable car 1877m |
| **Distance** | 10km |
| **Time** | 4hr 30min |
| **Terrain** | Small mountain trails with one short section of scrambling |
| **High point** | Aiguille du Belvédère 2965m |
| **Altitude gain** | 600m |
| **Map** | Top 25 3630 OT Chamonix Mont Blanc |
| **Parking** | La Flégère cable car, Les Praz |

The Aiguille du Belvédère is one of the highest peaks of the Aiguilles Rouges, situated towards the northern end of the range, directly above Lac Blanc, and it is certainly well named. Of course, pretty much everything on this north-west side of the valley enjoys views of Mont Blanc, but this mountain seems to be blessed with one of the best panoramas, probably enhanced by the delightful ascent route. The way to the top, though not outrageously hard, has one short section which is at the high end of what can be defined as 'walking', entailing a short but quite fierce rocky scramble where a determined pull or two are necessary to make progress. Coming down, careful footwork and perhaps some teamwork are key.

From the top of the **Index** chairlift take the trail which heads north-east across the southern slopes of the Aiguille Crochues, to the **Chalet du Lac Blanc**. Go around the **Lac Blanc** and take a cairned path up rocky ground towards the **Col des Dards**. This slope will be névé at some point and there will almost always be a decent track coming from the Aiguille Crochues.

Just before reaching the Col des Dards, head up right, usually on snow, to join a rocky rib. This rib leads to the main south ridge of **Aiguille du Belvédère**. Follow this to a steep but short chimney (20m, grade III). Beyond this, easy scrambling again leads to the steep rocky summit

# ❸ Aiguille du Belvédère

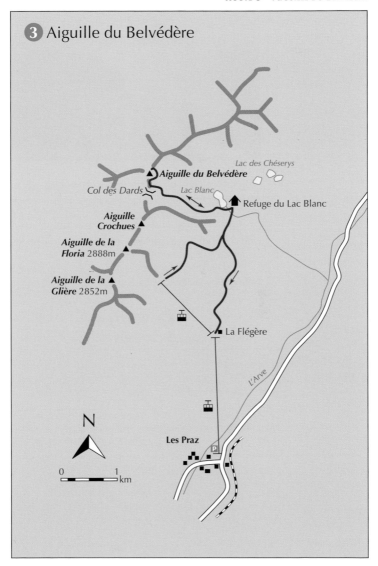

*Lac des Chéserys*

▲ ***Aiguille du Belvédère***

*Col des Dards*

*Lac Blanc*

🔺 Refuge du Lac Blanc

**Aiguille Crochues** ▲

**Aiguille de la Floria** 2888m ▲

**Aiguille de la Glière** 2852m ▲

🚡

■ La Flégère

🚡

*L'Arve*

**Les Praz**

🅿

N

0    1
km

*Sharing the broad
summit of the
Belvédère with the
locals*

block – a geological curiosity, being a limestone cap on the granite of the Aiguilles Rouges range. Luckily, a footpath in the red earthy terrain leads around to the right towards the north ridge. Now easy scrambling up this (and sometimes just to its left) leads to the top, with the actual summit a little further on.

Descend by the same route to Lac Blanc then take the wide and frequented trail back to the Flégère cable car.

 **ROUTE 4**

*Mer de Glace Balcony Trail*

| | |
|---|---|
| **Start/Finish** | Montenvers 1909m |
| **Distance** | 15km – this varies slightly according to the line taken up the glacier |
| **Time** | Time 8h+ In summer (2022) the Montenvers train runs from 8h30 to 17h30, which barely gives time to complete this walk in the day. Best to book a night at the hut or be ready to turn around before you get there. |
| **Terrain** | Mountain trails, steps, glacier walking, moraine paths, boulders, ice, ladders; the terrain is often demanding, physical and tiring. A harness and via ferrata leash and/or rope are essential to safely ascend and descend the ladders. A helmet is also highly recommended. Crampons will aid progress on the icy sections of the glacier. |
| **High point** | 2858m |

| | |
|---|---|
| **Altitude gain** | Around 1000m – the undulations on the trail are difficult to calculate |
| **Map** | Top 25 3630 OT Chamonix Mont Blanc |
| **Parking** | Montenvers railway station or Les Planards opposite |
| **Note** | Montenvers is at 1909m, at the terminus of its own rack, and pinion railway, which comes from its own station in Chamonix. This is not to be confused with the main Chamonix train station nearby. |
| **Warning** | This route crosses terrain that is contantly changing. The Mer de Glace glacier is shrinking at an alarming rate and this means that access to it is progressively more difficult. Years of warming temperatures mean that there is a risk of rockfall from the steep sides of the glaciated valley and the trail has been affected. The route described here is a shorter version of that previously known as the Mer de Glace Balcony Route, because longer versions risk being closed or altered. **Before embarking on this adventurous expedition it is essential that you check on viabilty at the OHM office (La Chamoniarde) in Chamonix.** |

The full version of this unique trail provides a spectacular circuit of the refuges of the Mer de Glace, but the balcony section from the Mer de Glace to the Couvercle Refuge is in itself a great objective. The scenery is nothing short of magnificent. The ladders that lead up to the balcony path are impressive and long. After that the trail along the hillside is intermittently equipped with ladders, rungs and cables, leading to the Couvercle Refuge.

The route described here is an out and back along the balcony trail from Montenvers. The IGN map shows the 2015 ladders to the Charpoua and Couvercle huts correctly marked, but it also shows the old ladders opposite Montenvers, which are no longer maintained. Equally the ladders down from Montenevers via the Vire des Guides are no longer there, and the descent from the Couvercle via les Egralets has been repositioned.

It is easy to underestimate this hike. It is a serious and arduous expedition and the terrain is difficult. Crampons, harness, via ferrata leash and helmet are essential. The ladders are equipped with protection points for those who choose to rope up. If you miss the last train down you'll be faced with a long walk back to Chamonix.

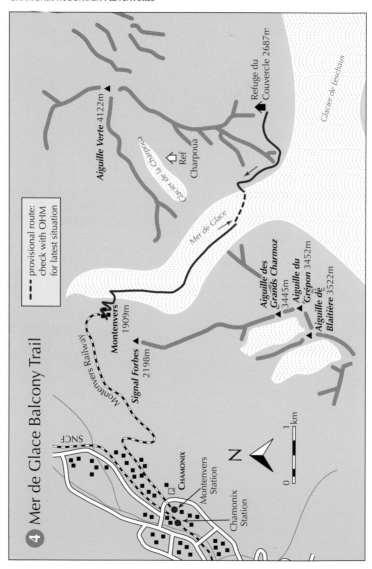

**4** Mer de Glace Balcony Trail

From **Montenvers**, at the time of writing, the only way down to the **Mer de Glace** is to go down to the Grotte de Glace. This can be accessed by a cable car and then via several hundred steps. The cable car opens some time after the arrival of the first train, so if you arrive early take the footpath to the left of the cable car, looking out, to reach the steps. There are plans for a new cable car which should go all the way to the glacier, but this is in the early stages of construction.

*The impressive ladders leading up to the balcony trail*

Previously there was a long ladder descent from Montenvers arriving further up the glacier (La Vire des Guides), but as of 2022 this has been taken down.

Once you arrive at the **Grotte de Glace** you need to take the easiest way up the glacier. At this level the glacier is largely composed of rocks on ice, and can be quite tortuous. Especially early morning, the icy sections will be slippery and care should be taken. Crampons will most likely be usefuland it is advisable to try to see where others have gone before...tracks in the dust, the odd cairn....otherwise you risk finding very loose ground. After leaving this rather chaotic section, the way gets

141

more obvious and there is a choice: either go left across a glacier stream onto ice and go along there, or stay on the moraine in the centre of the glacier. The latter is the safest option as you do not cross the river, which has quite steep sides and you stay well away from the steep rocky sides of the valley, which can be prone to rockfall.

However, walking up moraine is tricky and takes time. After about 2hr of walking you reach the area marked on the map as **Les Moulins**. The 'moulins' are the water channels formed in the ice by running water. Keep looking up left and you should spot the ladders, high up on the granite slabs. You might also spot cairns with red markers but these are few and far between and easy to miss. This is the access route for the Charpoua Refuge as well as the Couvercle. The ladder route is marked with a big yellow square, which is way up the cliff, and it begins at 2060m. To reach the base of the ladders make your way across the streams and onto the moraine scree. Again, look carefully for the most worn way up this, following waymarks if you're lucky.

The ladders are long and steep. Every few metres there is a fixed bolt and carabine, which is for use when you are roped up to someone. There are small ledges from time to time where you can rest, or allow others to pass coming the other way. It is not safe to climb these ladders unattached. If not using ropes then you need to use a via ferrata leash. There is a good chance of small rocks coming down from people ahead so a helmet is a very good idea.

After the ladders, the path continues into grassy terrain with chains and cables to help. Eventually you reach the junction where the Charpoua trail goes left and the onwards trail to the **Couvercle Hut** goes right. This well waymarked path (red flashes and yellow squares) is now easier, but there are numerous undulations and another series of ladders – take it steady and savour the stunning situation – glaciers and soaring rocky peaks as far as you can see. The path arrives just below the Couvercle Refuge at a big cairn – about 1hr30 from the top of the access climb. In hot conditions there can be water pouring down some of the gullies traversed so expect to get a soaking.

Return by the same route. Be sure to allow plenty of time for the return (at least as much as your outward journey) – the endless steps back up from the Grotte de Glace are fairly painful, although not as painful as the disappointment of missing the last train back down to Chamonix.

 ## ROUTE 5

*Tré-les-Eaux Circuit*

| | |
|---|---|
| **Start** | Le Couteray 1360m |
| **Finish** | Emosson 1965m |
| **Distance** | 14km |
| **Time** | 8hr |
| **Terrain** | Mountain paths, cabled rocky passage and pathless sections marked by cairns. Note that this cabled path is not on the current (2002) IGN map. A much shorter circuit is possible: from the top of the equipped section of trail, a path heads back right and eventually leads down to the start point. This path is on the map, marked in places with dots as a difficult path, but it is fairly straightforward. |
| **High point** | Col des Corbeaux 2602m |
| **Altitude gain** | 1450m |
| **Map** | Top 25 3630 OT Chamonix Mont Blanc |
| **Parking** | Le Couteray |

The Tré-les-Eaux valley is a secret gem – far les frequented than its popular neighbour, the Bérard valley. This might be because the trail alongside the river in the Tré-les-Eaux is blocked some way up by imposing rocky slabs. However, for those looking for a bit of zest, this provides the excitement of the route – those rocky slabs are overcome by means of metal cables and rungs, allowing access to the rest of the valley, a wild and spectacular delight. A long ascent leads over the Col des Corbeaux to the Vieux Emosson cirque and a foray over to the dinosaur tracks (Family Walks, Route 10), before descending the scenic Veudale gorge to Emosson Lake. (See page 27 for information about the construction works around the Emosson Lakes area.) A long and very special mountain day.

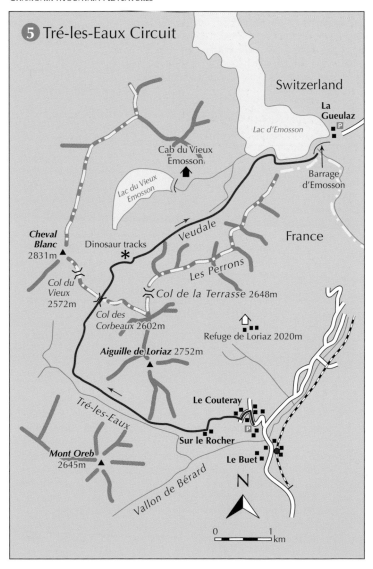

**5** Tré-les-Eaux Circuit

Switzerland

La Gueulaz

*Lac d'Emosson*

Cab du Vieux Emosson

*Lac du Vieux Emosson*

Barrage d'Emosson

*Cheval Blanc* 2831m

Dinosaur tracks

*Veudale*

France

Les Perrons

*Col de la Terrasse* 2648m

*Col du Vieux* 2572m

*Col des Corbeaux* 2602m

Refuge de Loriaz 2020m

*Aiguille de Loriaz* 2752m

*Tré-les-Eaux*

Le Couteray

Sur le Rocher

*Mont Oreb* 2645m

Le Buet

*Vallon de Bérard*

N

0    1 km

From **Le Couteray** a good trail winds up through the forest, west, to the tiny hamlet of **Sur le Rocher**. The **Tré-les-Eaux** valley is signed from here. The trail wanders along next to the babbling river until forced to break away up to an obvious area of golden rocky cliffs. Chains then cables up the prominent chimney corner provide a fun ascent – for those who like that sort of thing.

At the top a short descent leads back towards the valley, nevertheless staying high above the river on a series of wide rocky ramps and ledges. Another short section is protected by chains, then the trail becomes easier. From hereon there are no more equipped sections, but the path climbs steeply and fairly relentlessly out of the valley to reach the **Col des Corbeaux** (2602m), with impressive views of the brooding East Face of Mont Buet.

*The equipped section of the Tré-les-Eaux trail is exciting but not too scary*

Once at the col, pick up a cairned descent route northwards to reach better a better trail at the **dinosaur tracks**. Beyond the footprints, continue north-east up zig-zags to the top of the **Veudale** gorge then follow the all-too-obvious path all the way down and along this enticing valley. At the exit there will be some sort of walkway leading to the café and car park at Emosson. To return to Le Couteray, take the bus or cable car/funicular to Le Châtelard, then the train to Le Buet. Le Couteray is 5min from Le Buet.

**ROUTE 6**

*Loriaz to Emosson*

| | |
|---|---|
| **Start** | Le Couteray 1360m |
| **Finish** | Le Buet 1350m or Emosson 1965m |
| **Distance** | 12km, or 6.5km if the funicular and train are used |
| **Time** | 6hr |
| **Terrain** | The trails are all good but the traverse can get slippery in wet weather. Early in the season there are numerous shady gullies on the traverse that hold névé and are very dangerous, so even if there doesn't look to be any snow on the slopes, beware – this route is not usually in condition before early July. There is a bus service from the dam to Le Châtelard, as an alternative to the cable car/funicular option. |
| **High point** | Loriaz 2020m |
| **Altitude gain** | 800m |
| **Map** | Top 25 3630 OT Chamonix Mont Blanc |
| **Parking** | Le Couteray |

The ascent to the Loriaz Refuge is described fully in Hut Walks, Route 8. This extension from the hut to the Emosson Lake is one of the best balcony walks in the area – with a twist: there are several sections of metal handrail and a few chains to ensure safe passage. This is far from being a via ferrata, and in dry conditions you'll probably not even use every aid point, but these sections add excitement to the walk and make it a memorable hike. A steep but picturesque trail leads down from the Emosson dam to Barberine in the Vallorcine valley, followed by a gentle walk back up to Le Couteray. Alternatively, to add to the adventure, it would be fun to take the cable car/funicular ride down from Emosson to Le Châtelard then the train back up to Le Buet.

This is the shortest Adventure Walk contained in the book (especially if combined with the funicular/train) and can be done by people who wouldn't necessarily like some of the longer walks in this section. Children who are used to hiking rough trails could be taken along here, but should be looked after and not put out in front.

From **Le Couteray** take the forest track then footpath up to the **Refuge de Loriaz** (see Hut Walks, Route 8). From

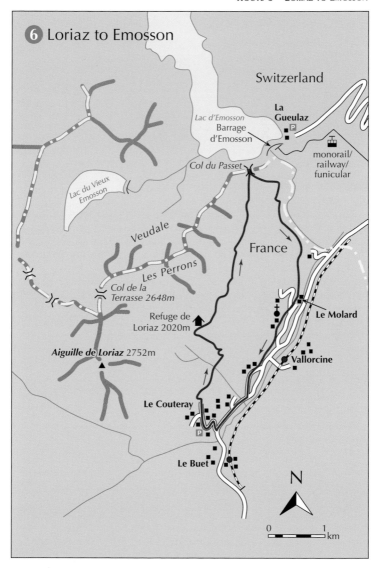

**6** Loriaz to Emosson

Switzerland

La Gueulaz

*Lac d'Emosson*
Barrage
d'Emosson

monorail/
railway/
funicular

*Col du Passet*

*Lac du Vieux
Emosson*

*Veudale*

France

Les Perrons

*Col de la
Terrasse 2648m*

Refuge de
Loriaz 2020m

Le Molard

*Aiguille de Loriaz* 2752m

Vallorcine

Le Couteray

Le Buet

N

0          1
km

147

*The first part of the trail from Loriaz to Emosson is easy. Behind is the whole massif from Mont Blanc past the Chamonix Aiguilles to the Drus and the Verte, with the Dent du Géant in the far distance*

the hut the balcony path sets off north-east and it's just a question of staying on it. There are infrequent yellow and orange-and-red paint flashes but these are not necessary as there are no proper path junctions, just some climbers' trails here and there off to the left.

The way is fairly easy to begin with. Later, numerous sections of trail have rocky steps, and chains and cables are encountered on some parts.

Well before reaching it you'll see the **Emosson Lake** and it seems really close, but the path has a few undulations to make the way seem quite tiring and it will take longer than you expect to do the final part. There is a good view of the red cable car that descends above the far end of the dam to link up with the railway running around the hillside into a tunnel. This is the descent route from the dam if you choose not to walk down.

At the **Col du Passet** just before the lake there is a signpost which indicates a steep trail going south, down to Vallorcine and this trail should be taken unless you've decide on the funicular option. (If you're taking the funicular, follow the signed route to the other side of the dam and go up to the top of the red cable car).

The trail down from the Col du Passet is rocky and steep at first but the terrain soon eases and becomes more stable as the route weaves its way around cliffs and over streams. Just before the path on the left to the Cascade de Barberine, take a right turn to **Le Molard** (signed to Vallorcine). Go through Le Molard and up by the church to pick up the Chemin des Diligences to Le Nant. Then go through Le Morzay and along the road to the turning right to Le Couteray.

 # ROUTE 7

*Mont Buet by the North Ridge*

| | |
|---|---|
| **Start/Finish** | Le Buet 1350m |
| **Distance** | 4.5km to the hut; 15km next day to the summit and down |
| **Time** | 1hr 30min to the hut; 8hr the next day. |
| **Terrain** | Excellent trail to the hut, rocky trail towards the Col de la Terrasse. Well-maintained paths, with chains near the top of Cheval Blanc, all the way to Cheval Blanc then vague across to Col Genévrier. The north ridge is airy with cables. The descent requires some concentration at times, but is very well used. This route should not be attempted in early summer because of the risk of névé. |
| **High point** | Mont Buet 3096m |
| **Altitude gain** | 670m to the hut; about 1320m the next day to the summit |
| **Map** | Top 25 3630 OT Chamonix Mont Blanc |
| **Parking** | Le Buet |

Mont Buet, or *le Mont Blanc des dames* as it is known locally, is an extremely fine and sought-after summit. Justifiably so as it is the highest peak in the Aiguilles Rouges range and also provides one of the finest belvederes – from Mont Blanc all the way around past the Aravis, the Rochers des Fiz, Mont Ruan, the Tour Sallière and the rest of the Alps.

The normal route is long and pretty hard work – that will be the descent route here. Traversing the summit by the north ridge gives a hike of great interest and variety and allows you to discover this mountain in all its glory. You also get to climb the stunning Cheval Blanc en route, described as Adventure Walk in its own right in Adventure Walks, Route 8.

I strongly recommend that a night is spent at the Refuge de Loriaz so as to get a really early start for the summit day – the walk from hut to summit, and even more so the descent, should not be underestimated.

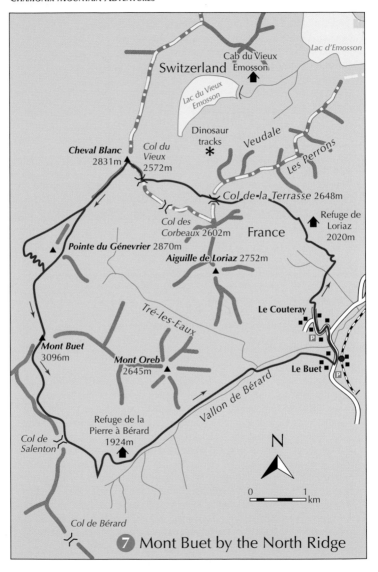

Switzerland

Cab du Vieux
Emosson

Lac d'Emosson

Lac du Vieux
Emosson

Dinosaur
tracks
✳

Veudale

Les Perrons

**Cheval Blanc**
2831m

*Col du
Vieux*
2572m

*Col de la Terrasse* 2648m

*Col des
Corbeaux* 2602m

**France**

Refuge de
Loriaz
2020m

▲ **Pointe du Génevrier** 2870m

**Aiguille de Loriaz** 2752m ▲

*Tré-les-Eaux*

**Le Couteray**

**Mont Buet**
3096m ▲

**Mont Oreb** ▲
2645m

**Le Buet**

*Vallon de Bérard*

Refuge de la
Pierre à Bérard
1924m

*Col de
Salenton*

N

0          1
km

*Col de Bérard*

**7** Mont Buet by the North Ridge

From **Le Buet** walk down the road to the turn off left to **Le Couteray** then go up to this hamlet. Keep going up the road until a track goes off to the right, signed to Loriaz Refuge. Take this then the footpath signed to **Loriaz**, up to the hut (see Hut Walks, Route 8).

From the hut a clear trail sets off behind the hut (north-west). At first grassy, this trail becomes rocky and steep higher up and is increasingly loose as it nears the **Col de la Terrasse** (2648m).

Once at the col it is best to head down north-west following cairns to a junction just above the dinosaur tracks at around 2400m where you then take a traverse west under the slopes of the Pointe de Corbeaux to reach the **Col du Vieux** (2572m). The trail is obvious up the **Cheval Blanc** (2831m), protected by a few chains at the top. Once on this summit the views are already magnificent but this peak is described later (Adventure Walks, Route 8).

The next part of the walk takes a vague path, which is easy to miss, heading south-west under the **Pointe du Génevrier** to the unmarked col on the far side (2808m). There are cairns from time to time and the occasional red paint mark, but if the cloud came down it could seem very serious. (If there is névé on the east slopes of the Pointe du Génevrier then an alternative route

*The exciting North Ridge of Mont Buet*

exists from the Col du Génevrier down to the west side of the Pointe du Génevrier to the Plan du Buet where you'll meet a good trail coming up from the Giffre valley. This trail goes up to the unnamed col). The route up the north ridge starts here and is impressive but fairly short, with several sections of cable interspersed with easy rocky steps. The view back along the ridge is particularly remarkable. Soon you'll reach the almost flat summit shoulder, which gives a final gentle stroll along to the summit of **Mont Buet**, marked by a large cairn and, most likely, lots of people.

To descend, take the broad south-west shoulder for about 500m before the path descends left past a small col at 2700m. The trail onwards is marked by cairns and red paint flashes – it goes through rocky ground under the **Col de Salenton** before becoming more distinct and zigzagging down to the **Refuge de la Pierre à Bérard** – time for a welcome beer before the easier walk out down the Bérard valley back to Le Buet.

 **ROUTE 8**

*Cheval Blanc*

| | |
|---|---|
| **Start/Finish** | La Guelaz 1965m |
| **Distance** | 15.5km |
| **Time** | 6–7hr |
| **Terrain** | Good mountain paths with just a short section of chains to attain the summit |
| **High point** | Cheval Blanc 2831m |
| **Altitude gain** | 866m |
| **Map** | Top 25 3630 OT Chamonix Mont Blanc |
| **Parking** | La Guelaz at Emosson |
| **Note** | For those looking for an adrenaline rush there is now a very long and spectacular tyrolien (Pures Emossions) on offer from the Emosson restaurant! |

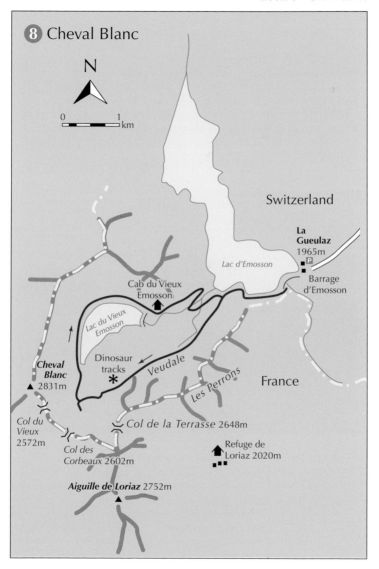

**❽ Cheval Blanc**

N

0        1 km

Switzerland

**La Gueulaz**
1965m

*Lac d'Emosson*

Barrage
d'Emosson

Cab du Vieux
Emosson

*Lac du Vieux
Emosson*

**Cheval
Blanc**
▲ 2831m

Dinosaur
tracks
✳

*Veudale*

Les Perrons

France

*Col du
Vieux*
2572m

*Col de la Terrasse* 2648m

*Col des
Corbeaux* 2602m

Refuge de
Loriaz 2020m

**Aiguille de Loriaz** 2752m
▲

The Cheval Blanc summit stands proud above the south end of the Vieux Emosson Lake, a sentinel guarding the Franco-Swiss frontier. There is an exciting feeling of remoteness on this peak, despite the nearby presence of the lake and various pylons scattered around. From the summit the northern slopes plunge down to the Giffre valley, a steep rocky void far below, and ibex are very often to be seen roaming the slopes to the south-west.

Most of this walk is just that, a walk, but right at the top a series of chains provide reassuring handholds to overcome the last steep steps. The views down to the lake are almost vertiginous and this certainly qualifies as 'adventurous'.

*On the final ridge of Cheval Blanc, with the Emosson Lakes below*

From **Emosson** follow the walkway across the dam and find the well-maintained trail to **Veudale** on the left. This scenic valley provides initially gentle climbing through grassy slopes populated by marmots, under golden cliffs, before steeper rocky terrain at the top. Once you exit the gorge the views of the Vieux Emosson Lake are quite surprising and the Cheval Blanc is easily recognisable above the far end of the lake. A zigzag path leads

down a steepish slope and over past the **dinosaur tracks** (Family Walks, Route 10). Just beyond is a signpost. Go right and take a clearly defined traverse to the **Col du Vieux** (2572m) from where the summit path is obvious and well maintained.

*Looking down to the Giffre valley from the summit of Cheval Blanc*

Descend by the same route to the signpost. Then take the wide trail that contours around the south side of the **Vieux Emosson Lake**. After the **Cabane du Vieux Emosson** a narrow tarmac road leads down to the main Emosson road and the walkway will be picked up to return to the car park. At the time of writing there is a shuttle bus service from this road junction to the car park.

155

# 🚶 TRAIL RUNNING

*The race everyone dreams of – the Ultra Trail du Mont Blanc*

In recent years trail running has taken off in Chamonix, partly because running off-road is increasingly popular in all mountain areas and also because, since 2003, Chamonix has hosted the Ultra Trail du Mont Blanc (UTMB), arguably Europe's most prestigious trail running ultra (longer than marathon distance) race.

Several races take place during the summer months on the Chamonix valley trails. The main races are listed in this chapter and it's worth knowing the dates of these so as not to choose to be walking on a race route on the day – the runners will be very focused and not terribly keen on giving way to anyone else. On the other hand, rather than avoiding those trails you might want to go and spectate or, even better, take part.

Whether or not races are your goal, any keen runner visiting Chamonix will almost certainly want to lace up his or her trainers, don a small hydration sack and take off for a run, be it alongside the Arve in the warm larch forest, or up to one of the high meadows with Mont Blanc as a back drop.

Running the trails is a quite different experience to walking them – the runner is lightweight, usually just out for an hour or two, able to get in a circuit before work or indeed before a walk with the family. Runners don't just stare at the trail ahead of them; they, too, admire the views, listen to the birdsong, feel the early morning dew and breathe the scent of forest and flowers.

Trail running in the Chamonix valley is renowned largely because of the magnificent stage on which it takes place – even on the UTMB numerous runners take cameras and will stop and stare and draw renewed strength from their surroundings.

## WHERE TO RUN

Many of the walks described in this book lend themselves to running, although the adventure and alpine walks are the exception to that. To qualify as a pleasant running route a trail should not be too steep, should be easy to navigate and reasonably well maintained, without nasty drop-offs ready to exact a price from a careless footstep. The trails in the Chamonix and Vallorcine valleys provide excellent, fairly gentle outings of around 10–15km. The Grand Balcons are also eminently runnable, as are the ascents to the Flégère, Balme and Posettes cable cars.

Equally the hut walks can make good runs, with the added advantage that once there you can be sure of refreshments.

## GEAR

- **Water** On many routes there are water sources (fountains, streams or indeed cafés), but it's still essential to take some drink – either in a handheld bottle or in a hydration pack.
- **Jacket** The weather can change suddenly in the mountains so some form of windproof top is a minimum requirement when running above the valley.

*Running with a backdrop of the Mont Blanc massif*

- **Mobile phone** This is highly recommended – a fall on some of these rough trails could easily leave you unable to walk out.
- **Poles** More and more mountain runners now use very lightweight poles and these can be extremely useful if the terrain is technical. They are allowed in certain races but not all.

Be sure to let someone know where you're going, especially if you're heading out for an evening run when an incident would mean you wouldn't be back by nightfall.

### FIVE OF THE BEST TRAIL RUNS

These runs take routes described in the walks in this guide, or variations on those walks, so there are no independent sketch maps given – it's important to refer to the relevant walk and get the details from there. No times are given because runners' paces are very variable. However, be aware that the ascents in the Alps may be longer than you're used to, the altitude can make itself felt and also the trails are sometimes rough and rocky. All these factors mean that the time taken to run a trail in the Alps could be longer than expected, so allow a bit of leeway, especially if going out at the end of the day.

### Chamonix Valley Circuit

This is a mix of various routes on foot and on mountain bike in this guide, but the basic itinerary is given here. Work it out on the map then follow your nose.

*Running up at the Refuge Loriaz is as good as it gets*

## MAIN RACES IN THE CHAMONIX REGION AND BEYOND

The events noted here are established races but there will be new ones each year. The dates are subject to change – check the internet.

*The prestigious Chamonix marathon finishes within sight of Mont Blanc at Planpraz (photo: Patricia Loffi)*

- **Mont Blanc Marathon** Marathon distance, with 2511m of ascent, also associated races – including the **Cross du Mont Blanc**, 23km with 1454m of ascent, which has existed longer than the marathon. Usually the last weekend of June. The same weekend there is also the **Kilometre Vertical**, which takes a 2km trail of tight zigzags under the Planpraz lift from Chamonix. The finish is as for the Marathon and the Cross.
- **Montagn'hard** is an ultra race of 108km with 8000+m of ascent. This event takes place in the Contamines Montjoie St Gervais mountains and runners ascend the scenic Mont Joly. There are also a number of shorter alternatives. Takes place in July.
- **La Montée du Nid d'Aigle** This one's an old classic, going from Le Fayet in the Arve valley all the way to the high point of the Tramway du Mont

159

Blanc. Variously cited as 19 or 20km and 1900 or 2000m of ascent, it takes places mid-July.
- **Trail du Tour des Fiz** and its smaller 'Petit' version. Starts at Plaine Joux and follows the Tour des Fiz; 63km with 5300m or 30km and 2400m. July.
- **UTMB** is the iconic race of the region, arguably the most famous in the world of trail running. 171km and 10,000m of ascent and descent. This race circumnavigates the Mont Blanc massif following the iconic Tour du Mont Blanc trail. Held during the last week of August, sign-up is on a points system with a lottery draw – the race is heavily over-subscribed each year.
- **CCC, TDC, OCC** and the **PTL (and maybe even others now)** are shorter races associated with the UTMB, also held during the last week of August.
- **Trail des Aiguilles Rouges** This race route varies slightly each year but it always some form of traverse of the Aiguilles Rouges and is about 50km with some 4000m of ascent. September.

**Races outside the area but feasible from Chamonix base**
- **Trail Faverge** In the Bauges area, not far from Annecy. An old classic, 42km and 2700m of ascent, with a shorter version. Mid-June.
- **La Combloranne** has three races of different lengths and takes place mid June.
- **Aravis Trail** features various versions, the longest of which is 67km and 4700m of ascent. June.
- **Trail du Gypaete** Organised by the town of Nancy sur Cluses, this June event has grown very fast and there are four races at the last count.
- **Ultra Trail du Haut-Giffre** This relatively new event is fast becoming a must-do for those looking for what seems to be longest race in the region of Samoëns Sixt Fer de Cheval. 124km, but with several shorter versions.
- **Trail des Glières** Races later in the year are relatively rare so this October event is unusual. There are three versions: 47km, 20km and 11km – something for everyone.

From Chamonix Place Mont Blanc take the track out right (north) alongside the River Arve to the main road coming from Chamonix to Les Praz. Soon after, leave the road on a track going along the other side of the river, to the Paradis des Praz. Continue straight on up the valley, mainly following the river to reach Argentière. Turn right past the Post Office and past the church, then take the back road to Montroc and up to Le Planet. Follow signs for Petit Balcon Nord, which is followed to Le Lavancher. Turn left uphill on the road in Le Lavancher to pick up a path on the right which is then signed all the way back to Chamonix.

### Refuge Bel Lachat

It's a long climb from Chamonix, but that's what trail runners do in the Alps. Once you hit your rhythm it goes quite steadily. This is the descent route in Hut Walks, Route 4. Probably best done as a there-and-back route when running, but if your knees are getting tired of descents you could go on up to the Brévent then take the lift down

### Chalet du Lac Blanc

There are various ways to run to Lac Blanc, but a good challenging route is from the Col des Montets by the steep zigzag trail to La Remuaz,

past the Lacs des Chéserys. From the hut take the big trail onwards to La Flégère, then save the knees by taking the cable car down. From Les Praz there is a bus service back up to the Col des Montets. See Classic Walks, Route 9.

### Aiguillette des Posettes

This wonderful belvedere provides a superb run, especially if accessed via the Col des Posettes from Vallorcine. The route is described in reverse in Classic Walks, Route 8 but for running it's probably easier to do the ridge walk in descent as it has some steep steps that, when encountered in ascent, would probably reduce most runners to walkers.

### Refuge de Loriaz

This a beautiful run, whether the hut is open or not. You can run up the nicely graded forest piste and then descend the footpath as described in Hut Walks, Route 8.

*Early morning descent in the Aiguilles Rouges*

# 2 ALPINE MOUNTAINEERING

*This is what alpine walking and climbing is all about (photo: Nigel Jones)*

Chamonix is home to some of the fiercest climbs in the Alps, but there are also some classic glacier walks and 'easy' alpine climbs that are feasible for any enthusiastic walker who has had appropriate training or is accompanied by a qualified guide or experienced friend. These routes will give glorious mountain experiences, in stunning and magical surroundings, and could well provide the finale to an alpine holiday.

However, you don't want that to be a definitive finale. It cannot be overstated that walking on glaciers is dangerous and requires the knowledge and skills to choose a

good route and also to be able to effect a rescue if someone falls into a crevasse. This means walking and climbing roped together using good technique and being ready to react correctly in the event of a snow-bridge giving way or someone slipping into a crevasse. See Appendix D for advice about glacier travel and rescue.

Equally, the alpine climbs described here require experience in appropriate rope-work, which is quite different to the type of rope-work you would use for one-pitch bolted rock climbing or climbing at a climbing wall.

Describing all these techniques in detail goes beyond the scope of this guide, however, and there are various publications available on the subject. Nevertheless, even equipped with all the literature, it's still essential to have honed these skills in a safe environment outside before going out into the real icy crevassed and sheer rocky world of the high Alps where one mistake could have dreadful consequences.

Hiking and climbing magazines feature adverts for all sorts of courses on alpine techniques, or you can hire a professional High Mountain Guide to take you on your chosen route, and learn some techniques along the way (see 'How to hire a guide' in the main introduction to this book).

## DEFINITIONS

### Glacier walking

This entails travelling on a 'wet' (snow-covered) glacier. Despite the lack of technical terrain, you'll need all the appropriate equipment (rope, harness, ice-axe, crampons plus a crevasse rescue kit).

### Scrambling

This refers to that ill-defined grey area between walking and rock climbing. For the route described (Alpine Mountaineering, Route 5) you'll need a rope (single), harness plus a minimum of rock-climbing equipment. Rock boots are not needed.

### Mixed climbing

As the name suggests, the climbing is on a mix of rock and snow/ice. You'll

*Heading across the Trient Plateau (photo: Nigel Jones)*

Care should be taken

need the same gear as for scrambling with the addition of crampons and an axe.

## TIMES

The times given here are approximate. They can vary enormously with snow conditions, glacier conditions at different times of the season, or simply with each individual's acclimatisation or indeed efficiency on alpine ground. Remember, they are just a rough guide.

## DISTANCES

It doesn't seem appropriate to give distances for these walks and climbs as they are often on technical terrain, which isn't defined by kilometres.

## WARNING

The warming global temperatures of the last decades have taken their toll on the high mountains, and the consequences of this are now being seen on an unprecedented scale in the Alps. Many routes are becoming unfeasible in the height of summer, due to rockfall, melting ice and huge yawning crevasses where previously hard snow made passage quite straightforward. The routes described here will change – before any ascent in the Alps it is highly recommended that you seek up-to-date information about conditions locally. In Chamonix the best source is the Office de Haute Montagne www.chamoniarde.com.

**ROUTE 1**

*Champex to Le Tour*

| | |
|---|---|
| **Start** | At the top of the La Breya chairlift |
| **Finish** | Le Tour |
| **Grade** | F |
| **Time** | Day 1: 4hr; Day 2: 4–5hr to Le Tour |
| **Terrain** | Glacier walking |
| **High point** | Col Supérieur du Tour 3289m |
| **Altitude gain** | Day 1: 982m; Day 2: 191m |
| **Map** | IGN Top 25 3630OT Chamonix Mont Blanc |
| **Parking** | La Breya chairlift, Champex |
| **Hut** | Cabane du Trient 3170m |

This very pleasant outing is basically the first two days of the summer Haute Route (Chamonix to Zermatt) in reverse. Neither day is particularly long and therefore there is plenty of time to use public transport to get to Champex in Switzerland to start the trip or to retrieve a car afterwards. The chairlift to La Breya at Champex closes at lunchtime and also stops when there is no one on it.

### Day 1

From the restaurant at the top of the chairlift take the footpath signed to the **Cabane d'Orny**. This contours high above the valley and then enters a beautiful flat corrie with a meandering stream running through it – an obvious picnic place. Steeper zigzags at the back of the cwm gain a classic moraine ridge. The Orny hut is a short distance higher up, perched above a turquoise lake and the path goes right past the door, so it'd be a shame not to take a break here, too. Follow the path onwards until you are forced onto the **Glacier d'Orny** – if it is snow-covered you must rope up. Keeping to the right-hand side (true left) of the glacier, continue a short distance looking for a large cairn and sign marking the start of the final path to the **Trient hut** in the rocky buttress. The hut is hidden around the corner and is only seen at the last moment.

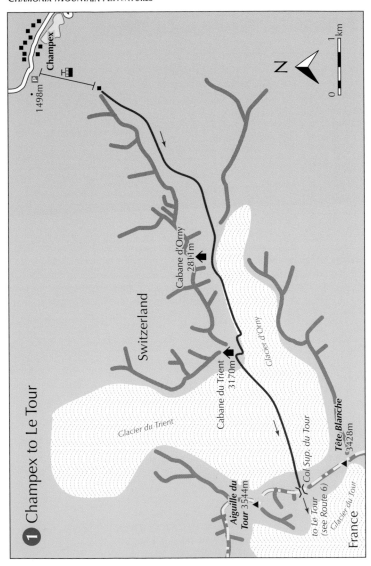

**1** Champex to Le Tour

Champex

1498m

Switzerland

Cabane d'Orny 2811m

Cabane du Trient 3170m

Glacier du Trient

Glacier d'Orny

Col Sup. du Tour

Aiguille du Tour 3544m

Tête Blanche 3428m

Glacier du Tour

to Le Tour (see Route 6)

France

N

0 — 1 km

**Day 2**

Walk down to the glacier and rope up. You are aiming to cross the **Col Supérieur du Tour** (3289m). The Col du Tour itself has become more and more difficult to pass on the Tour side over recent years due to glacial shrinkage and the Col Sup. has become the regular way. On the far side, a steepish slope leads down onto the **Tour Glacier**. There should be a good broad track to follow, working its way down to the right to the edge of the rocky slopes above the Albert Premier hut, where you can unrope. From the hut, the path leads down a moraine ridge and then veers right and around the corner. After this you have a choice – continue to the Col de Balme and take the chairlift, or walk down to Charamillon and take the cable car (or of course carry on walking down to Le Tour). If you value your knees don't be tempted to take the direct route to Le Tour, by continuing down the moraine from where the path veers right. (For the onward route from Col Supérieur du Tour see Alpine Mountaineering, Route 6.)

*On the way to the Col Supérieur du Tour (photo: Nigel Jones)*

# ROUTE 2

*Grands Montets to Lognan*

---

**IMPORTANT:**

The Grands Montets cable car is under reconstruction. As of summer 2022 the only lift open in this area is the Plan Joran télécabine, which runs during July and August. More information from the Chamonix website www.chamonix.com/informations-remontees-mecaniques-en-temps-reel. This makes the route a much longer proposition.

| | |
|---|---|
| **Start** | Top of the Grands Montets cable car 3295m |
| **Finish** | Lognan |
| **Grade** | F |
| **Time** | 4–5hr |
| **Terrain** | Glacier walking |
| **High point** | Aiguille des Grands Montets 3295m (top of cable car) |
| **Altitude gain** | 0m |
| **Map** | IGN Top 25 3630OT Chamonix Mont Blanc |
| **Parking** | Grands Montets cable car, Argentière |

This route is all downhill! It's a good walk in its own right but, given its brevity, it provides an ideal opportunity to learn glacier travel skills. The cable car takes you to almost 3300m and there will always be snow on the top part of the Rognons Glacier. In early season the snow will extend further down and the crevasses will be less evident. You must be roped up and equipped with glacier travel gear.

When you arrive at the top of the cable car, walk outside and go up the steps to the viewing platform. If this is your first day at this altitude you'll be out of breath, so walk slowly! The views in all directions from here are amazing. Having taken it all in, descend the long flight of steps to the **Col des Grands Montets** (3238m), and set foot on (hopefully) snow. Rope up here. Crampons will be needed – especially on a cold morning. The initial slope, down and over the bergschrund can be steep and intimidating,

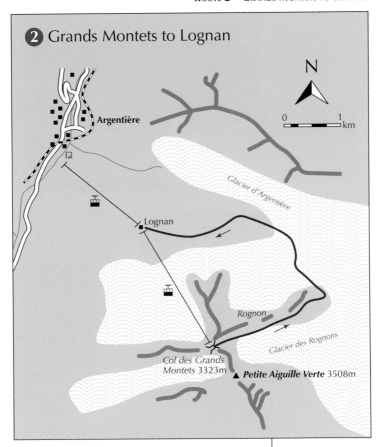

## ② Grands Montets to Lognan

Argentière

Glacier d'Argentière

Lognan

Rognon

Glacier des Rognons

Col des Grands
Montets 3323m  ▲ Petite Aiguille Verte 3508m

but it's only short and is often equipped with a fixed rope anchored to the rocks on its right side (looking down).

Easier slopes now lead down the glacier. You will probably encounter big crevasses after a couple of hundred metres, though in early season these will be hidden. Aim to pass to the right of the *rognon* (the big lump of rock sticking out of the glacier). Here the glacier steepens and maybe more complicated crevasses will be

*Impressive glacier scenery above the Argentière Glacier*

encountered. Aim for the top of a rock/moraine ridge directly in line with the rognon. You can leave the glacier and scramble along and then down this ridge, though it is just a little tricky in places. Access to the easy moraine ridge without scrambling along the rocky section is now very difficult due to spectacular glacial shrinkage in the last couple of years. Less problematic is to continue slightly right down the glacier for a short distance and set foot onto the smooth glaciated slabs and follow cairns to the left down these until a path is found in the moraine which leads to a junction with the Argentière hut path. Turn left and follow this across and down the rocky slopes, then, via a couple of ladders (rope children up, as they are quite steep), onto the **Argentière Glacier**. Normally this will be dry (snow-free) in the summer and you won't need to rope up.

Carry on down until a good path develops through the large jumbled boulders, and leads you onto the moraine ridge below the *Pointe de vue* (viewpoint). Don't be tempted to head directly up onto the ridge as the terrain is very unstable. A short descent on the crest of the ridge and you'll arrive at a tunnel entrance at the foot of the moraine. ◄

*The view of the seracs from here is very impressive.*

Alternatively, a wide stony track zigzags down to the left of the moraine. Follow the wide contouring track to **Lognan**.

## ROUTE 3

*Aiguille du Midi to Helbronner*

| | |
|---|---|
| **Start** | Aiguille du Midi 3842m |
| **Finish** | Helbronner lift station 3462m |
| **Grade** | F+ |
| **Time** | 3hr. Be aware that you may have to queue for the lift to get back. |
| **Terrain** | Glacier walking |
| **High point** | Aiguille du Midi 3840m |
| **Altitude gain** | About 250m from the lowest point of the traverse |
| **Map** | IGN Top 25 3630OT Chamonix Mont Blanc |
| **Parking** | Aiguille du Midi car park, Chamonix |

The traverse of the top of the 'Vallée Blanche' from the Aiguille du Midi to Pointe Helbronner gives *the* most scenic glacier walk in the Mont Blanc massif. Although it is completely non-technical, it does require the use of a rope, harness and crevasse rescue gear – and of course the know-how to go with it. There will nearly always be a track and it's highly unlikely you'll be alone. It is usual to return to the Aiguille du Midi using the red gondola lifts that link from Helbronner, so don't embark on the route if there's a storm forecast, as you'll be waiting for a bus back through the tunnel. Since the original publication of this book the Helbronner lift has been replaced by a fine new cable car known as the Skyway. However, the summit point is still Helbronner.

Descend the famous Midi Arête to easier ground, then work around to the right under the South Face of the Midi. The track will now split three ways. To the right is the Refuge des Cosmiques and the Cosmiques Arête; straight on is the normal route to Mont Blanc du Tacul and Mont Blanc; and to the left the way to Helbronner swings around in a wide gentle arc to the **Col du Gros Rognon** (3415m).

From the ill-defined col head down gentle slopes with the enormous crags of the East Face of Mont Blanc du Tacul towering above to your right. The easy slopes

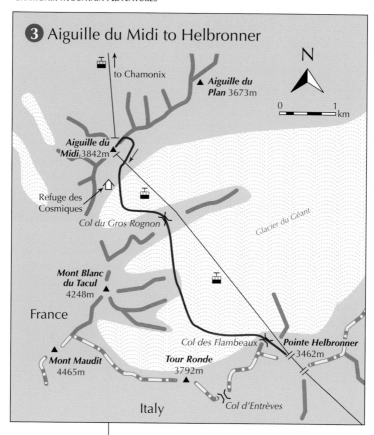

**3** Aiguille du Midi to Helbronner

to Chamonix

▲ *Aiguille du Plan* 3673m

N

0 ——— 1 km

*Aiguille du Midi* 3842m

Refuge des Cosmiques

*Col du Gros Rognon*

*Glacier du Géant*

*Mont Blanc du Tacul* 4248m

France

▲ *Mont Maudit* 4465m

*Tour Ronde* 3792m ▲

*Col des Flambeaux*

*Pointe Helbronner* 3462m

*Col d'Entrèves*

Italy

end at an impressive set of crevasses and seracs. Finding a way through here provides the crux of the route. Often the route can be very spectacular indeed and it's a place to keep your rope reasonably tight and expect the unexpected. Look up right occasionally to see the view of the incredibly impressive rock architecture of the Grand Capucin and other peaks unfolding.

After this section, the track will join the 'motorway' coming from the Tour Ronde and the Col d'Entrèves and

a short steep section leads to the **Col des Flambeaux** at 3407m. Once through here, the **Helbronner** lift station (3462m) is in sight, minutes away. Cappuccino in the café is a must.

*The ridge down from the Aiguille du Midi is quite memorable*

 **ROUTE 4**

*Petite Aiguille Verte*

---

**IMPORTANT:**

The Grands Montets cable car is under reconstruction. As of summer 2022 the only lift open in this area is the Plan Joran télécabine, which runs during July and August. More information from the Chamonix website www.chamonix.com/informations-remontees-mecaniques-en-temps-reel. This makes the route a much longer proposition.

| | |
|---|---|
| **Start/Finish** | Top of the Grands Montets cable car 3295m |
| **Grade** | PD |
| **Time** | 3hr |
| **Terrain** | Mixed climbing with a glacier approach |
| **High point** | Petite Aiguille Verte 3512m |

| | |
|---|---|
| **Altitude gain** | 273m |
| **Map** | IGN Top 25 3630OT Chamonix Mont Blanc |
| **Parking** | Grands Montets cable car, Argentière |

This is probably the most easily accessed little peak in the massif. It is generally done as a training/acclimatisation peak – however, it can be enjoyed in its own right, if only for its dramatic situation. As it is a half-day route, there's plenty of time to revise some alpine techniques … or just sit on the terrace with a beer.

On arrival at the top of the cable car climb up the steps to the viewing platform – this should make you puffed! Now look south-east and the huge mountain you'll see is the Aiguille Verte. Blending into its bulk is a much smaller peak – basically the first peak of the long Grands Montets ridge of the Aiguille Verte. You can see the whole of your proposed route from here – luxury!

*Big holes like this are best viewed from a distance!*

Descend the long flight of steps to the **Col des Grands Montets** (3238m) and rope up. Climb steepening slopes

with the odd crevasse, bearing right towards the very shortest and rightmost part of the little North Face. Climb over the bergschrund and up onto the ridge and follow this on a mix of snow and rock to the summit – rocky obstacles are generally turned on the left of the ridge, on the North Face of the **Petite Aiguille Verte**.

To descend, reverse the route. This route is often combined with the Grands Montets to Lognan route (Alpine Mountaineering, Route 2).

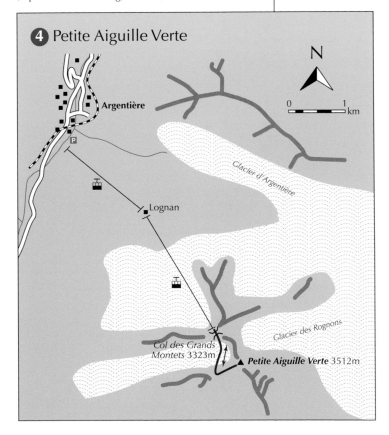

# ROUTE 5
*Aiguille Crochues*

| | |
|---|---|
| **Start** | Top of the Index chairlift 2385m |
| **Finish** | Top of La Flégère cable car 1877m |
| **Grade** | PD+ |
| **Time** | 7hr from top of Index lift to La Flégère, allowing time to enjoy the outing |
| **Terrain** | Scrambling on a rocky ridge with (often) a snow approach and descent |
| **High point** | Aiguille Crochues 2840m |
| **Altitude gain** | 455m |
| **Map** | IGN Top 25 3630OT Chamonix Mont Blanc |
| **Parking** | La Flégère cable car, Les Praz |

This is a classic Alpine rock ridge and with good reason. Not only is this climb of a very amenable standard, it is also superbly situated in the heart of the Aiguilles Rouges, with spectacular views to match, and so is very popular. It requires the whole range of Alpine rope-work appropriate to this sort of terrain.

Situated on the crest of the Aiguilles Rouges, the route benefits from quick and easy access and descent using the Flégère and Index lifts and can easily be done in a day without having a fraught end-of-day dash for the last cable car. A *combiné* ticket covering the Flégère and Index lifts in ascent and the Flégère lift in descent is available.

The route is easy to follow if you look out for the polish attesting to the generations of budding alpinists who have passed this way.

From the summit of the Index lift head towards the top of the short Floria ski-tow, then take the horizontal traversing path to almost below the East Face of the Crochues. Some steep zigzags now lead up to a short couloir which exits at the Col des Crochues. In early season this can all be on snow. From the col follow a short path that leads to the base of a 50m chimney on the west side of the ridge. Climb this at grade 3c. Now scramble up to the right onto the ridge and follow the crest on generally excellent rock. ◄

# ⑤ Aiguille Crochues

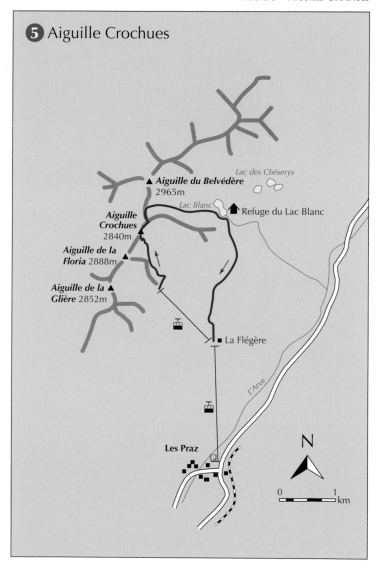

▲ *Aiguille du Belvédère*
2965m

Lac des Chéserys

Lac Blanc

🔺 Refuge du Lac Blanc

*Aiguille Crochues* 2840m ▲

*Aiguille de la Floria* 2888m ▲

*Aiguille de la Glière* 2852m ▲

■ La Flégère

L'Arve

**Les Praz**

N

0        1 km

*Taking a break on the Aiguille Crochues traverse*

Eventually you'll be forced to avoid a pinnacle on its right (east) side and arrive in a small notch. A short abseil from bolts leads to a ledge on the north side. Now regain the crest and follow it, passing from one side of the ridge to the other, until an easy scramble up right leads to the summit of the **Aiguille Crochues** – picnic time. Return to the main crest and follow this more easily to where it's possible to descend to snow slopes that usually give an easy and fast descent down to **Lac Blanc**. Follow everyone else now along the wide trail that returns to the top of the **Flégère cable car**.

 **ROUTE 6**

*Aiguille du Tour*

| | |
|---|---|
| **Start/Finish** | Top of the Le Tour (Balme) chairlift 2100m |
| **Grade** | F |
| **Time** | Day 1: 2hr; Day 2: 5hr hut to hut, then 1–2hr to Le Tour |
| **Terrain** | Mixed climbing with a glacier approach |
| **High point** | Aiguille du Tour 3544m |
| **Altitude gain** | From the hut 842m |
| **Map** | IGN Top 25 3630OT Chamonix Mont Blanc |
| **Parking** | Le Tour cable car |
| **Hut** | Refuge Albert Premier (Hut Walks, Route 6) |

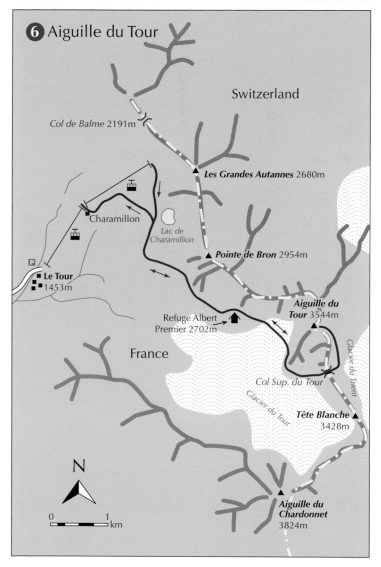

**6** Aiguille du Tour

Switzerland

*Col de Balme* 2191m

Charamillon

*Lac de Charamillion*

▲ *Les Grandes Autannes* 2680m

▲ *Pointe de Bron* 2954m

P

■ **Le Tour**
■■ 1453m

Refuge Albert
Premier 2702m

*Aiguille du
Tour* 3544m
▲

*Glacier du Trient*

France

*Col Sup. du Tour*

*Glacier du Tour*

*Tête Blanche* ▲
3428m

N

0          1
km

▲ *Aiguille du
Chardonnet*
3824m

The double-summited Aiguille du Tour is situated on the Franco-Swiss border dividing the Tour and Trient Glaciers, and is one of the most popular moderate alpine peaks in the Chamonix region. It is easily accessed from the Refuge Albert Premier and the proximity of this hut to the Balme chairlift combined with the reasonable grade of the climb mean that you're unlikely to be alone on this summit on any nice summer's day. However, it is a good training peak and also gives spectacular views of the Mont Blanc massif and interesting climbing.

*A great summit day on the Aiguille du Tour*

### Day 1
Though it is obviously possible to walk from Le Tour, most folk use the lift to either Charamillon (the mid station) or to the Col de Balme. Either way should see you at the hut in a couple of hours (see Hut Walks, Route 6).

### Day 2
Walk up the rocky slopes behind the hut for about 20min (you should have left the hut before dawn so you'll be in the dark, but there are numerous cairns) until you reach

the **Glacier du Tour**. Here you'll need to put on harness and crampons and rope up. The route makes its way to the right under the ridges of the peak until you can ascend to and cross the **Col Supérieur du Tour** (3289m) and gain the Trient Glacier. Take care not to mistake the Col Sup. glacier basin with the one further left (north), which leads to a harder route, the Couloir de la Table, but which doesn't offer a way through to the Trient Glacier. From the col, turn left and follow the edge of the glacier up quite a steep slope, just next to the crags, until you come to a flatter area under the summit rocks.

There are various ways to the summit of **Aiguille du Tour**, the easiest, most popular and most reliable being to cross the (sometimes quite large) bergschrund and make your way to the left arête where you can leave your axe and crampons if the rocks are dry. Now follow an easy line of weakness in the rocks a little way right and parallel to the arête until you arrive on the little north ridge just below the summit. Climb up steeper rocks to the top.

Descent is the ascent route in reverse.

 **ROUTE 7**

*The Cosmiques Arête*

| | |
|---|---|
| **Start/Finish** | Top of the Aiguille du Midi 3842m |
| **Grade** | AD |
| **Time** | 4hr |
| **Terrain** | Mixed climbing with a glacier approach |
| **High point** | Aiguille du Midi 3840m |
| **Altitude gain** | 250m |
| **Map** | IGN Top 25 3630OT Chamonix Mont Blanc |
| **Parking** | Aiguille du Midi car park, Chamonix |
| **Note** | A rockfall in 2018 changed the itinerary where there is a section of abseil. This section remains potentially unstable, especially in dry conditions, and care must be taken. Some older descriptions of the route do not take this into account. If in doubt ask at the OHM office and refer to this topo www.chamoniarde.com/images/files/Variante-Cosmiques-2019.jpg. |

This is a very easily accessible short mixed climb in a spectacular position. It has the advantage (or otherwise) of finishing at the top of the Aiguille du Midi cable car and is a must-have for any alpinist's CV. It can be (and is) climbed at any time of year and in most conditions, so there will nearly always be a track to follow.

At the end of the dark tunnel leading from the top of the cable car, turn left to exit through a blue ice cave. Descend the most famous arête in the Alps until you can swing around to the right onto the glacier to pass underneath the Aiguille du Midi's south face. Head slightly right towards the Refuge des Cosmiques, and then right again to the Abri Simond (a rather tatty bivouac shelter), when it comes into view. The start of the route is just a few metres from this hut.

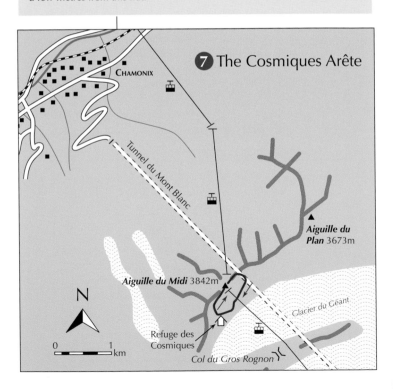

**7** The Cosmiques Arête

CHAMONIX

*Tunnel du Mont Blanc*

▲ *Aiguille du Plan* 3673m

*Aiguille du Midi* 3842m ▲

*Glacier du Géant*

Refuge des Cosmiques

*Col du Gros Rognon*

N

0   1 km

*The crux pitch of the Cosmiques Arête – short and sweet*

Climb easy cracks and chimneys and the occasional cracked slabs for a fair distance, then head slightly right before reaching a rocky pinnacle equipped with a bolted belay. From here an awkward diagonal abseil leads to a new abseil anchor at a col. Make an 8m abseil down the NW face. From here there are two options. It is possible to return to the SE face and to descend the chimney, to then climb up to reach a ledge on the right. But the preferred route, given the unstable rocks in that part of the SE face, is to go down and around the big block (rightwards facing out) and climb back up to regain the SE face. Go right again, then climb to easier ground on the ridge. Easy blocks lead right towards a large gendarme, which is turned on the right, followed by a short snow/ice slope to gain the ridge again, just before the crux wall. Surmount this either with a point of aid or by free climbing – using the chipped footholds.

Continue up easier rock on the right till a step left leads to a large flat ledge. Now go around left and down onto the shady side and climb a long, open chimney which leads up onto the ridge. A few more metres along the ridge and you'll see a ladder leading to the viewing platform and its dozens of admiring sightseers. Muster up as much dignity as you can and climb the ladder – don't trip over the balustrade …

# ROUTE 8
*Mont Blanc*

| | |
|---|---|
| **Start/Finish** | Nid d'Aigle 2372m, the terminus of the Tramway du Mont Blanc railway |
| **Grade** | PD+ |
| **Time** | Day 1: 5–6hr; Day 2: 6hr hut to hut, plus 4hr to the Nid d'Aigle |
| **Terrain** | Day 1: scrambling to the hut (helmet essential); Day 2, steep glacier and a narrow snow ridge |
| **High point** | Mont Blanc 4810m |
| **Altitude gain** | Day 1: 1445m; Day 2: 993m |
| **Map** | IGN Top 25 3531 ET Saint-Gervais-les-Bains |
| **Parking** | Bellevue cable car, Les Houches |
| **Hut** | Refuge du Goûter (Refuge de l'Aiguille du Goûter on the map). This big relatively new hut only takes reservations by internet. Demand is huge and you should usually reserve well ahead. |
| **Note** | The access route to the Refuge du Goûter (across the Grand Couloir) is dangerous due to regular rockfall. In hot years (notably 2022) this danger becomes so great that the route is officially closed. In addition, as of summer 2022, the route above the hut leading to the summit has changed due to the opening up of a large crevasse on the Arête des Bosses. For up to date information before embarking on this ascent it is essential to find out about current conditions from the Office de Haute Montagne www.chamoniarde.com. |

At 4810m (recently revised from 4807m), the highest point in western Europe needs little introduction. It has two *voies normales* (on the French side) – the Goûter Route and the slightly harder 'Traversée des Trois Monts' via the shoulders of Mont Blanc du Tacul and Mont Maudit from the Aiguille du Midi/Cosmiques hut. Described here is the former as it's less committing and has a shorter summit day. Despite it being the easier of the two, it shouldn't be underestimated. The approach to the hut on Day 1 has considerable objective dangers and the changing route on Day 2 will evolve in ways that cannot be speculated on here.

**Day 1**

Take the Bellevue cable car from Les Houches then walk a few hundred metres to the railway station and take the train to the **Nid d'Aigle**.

A broad footpath leads from here, via the Baraque Forestière des Rognes, to the **Refuge de Tête Rousse** (an alternative, if rather low, hut if the Goûter is full). Just before the hut you'll arrive at the small Tête Rousse Glacier. Follow a track across it to pass under the steep slopes of the **Aiguille du Goûter**.

Climb some easy rocks for a very short distance to the start of a traverse across the notorious Grand Couloir. This couloir is very exposed to stonefall (so wear a helmet) and should be crossed as early in the day as possible. Indeed, some people use the Tête Rousse hut as a starting point so that they cross it in the very early hours.

*Mont Blanc seen from the Cosmiques Arête*

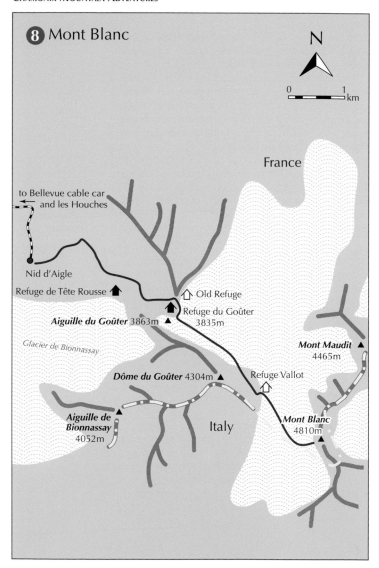

**8** Mont Blanc

N

0 _____ 1 km

France

to Bellevue cable car
and les Houches

Nid d'Aigle

Refuge de Tête Rousse

Old Refuge

Refuge du Goûter
3835m

*Aiguille du Goûter* 3863m ▲

*Glacier de Bionnassay*

Mont Maudit ▲
4465m

*Dôme du Goûter* 4304m ▲

Refuge Vallot

*Aiguille de Bionnassay*
4052m ▲

Italy

*Mont Blanc*
4810m ▲

Once across the couloir (which can be snow, ice or earth, depending on the season) a long rocky rib is gained which leads up to the hut, with sections of cable/handrail en route. There will be an extra short section to reach the new **Goûter hut**.

**Day 2**

From the hut climb the slopes of the **Dôme du Goûter**, passing to the left of its summit to arrive at the Col du Dôme. The **Refuge Vallot** stands just above at 4362m and provides shelter in case of bad weather or a place that a member of the party can be left if feeling the effects of altitude. This hut is an emergency shelter and should not be abused by planning a night there.

*That much desired summit shot (photo: Fred Ancey)*

*Descending the Dome de Goûter slope towards the hut with Chamonix in cloud below (photo: Caroline Ogden)*

Above the hut the Arête des Bosses snakes up to the summit of **Mont Blanc** 448 vertical metres above. The ridge is very narrow in places and care must be taken when stepping aside for people coming the other way. In 2022 a large crevasse opened up here and made the route significantly more difficult. It is impossible to give more details here at this time but the whole route could change again, so do inform yourself before heading out.

Descend by the same route.

# 3 MOUNTAIN BIKING

*Mountain biking near the Tour Glacier (photo: Marc Volorio)*

Mountain biking has been heavily promoted over the last few years in the Chamonix valley and there are now many dedicated mountain bike routes of different types: regular trails where you bike up and downhill to go from A to B; crazy downhill rides where you need to be fully equipped with body armour, but you don't need mountain lungs and legs as you get taken up by lift; or bike parks where generally young people ride over obstacles at great speed to get maximum airtime. This latter provides great spectator sport and also doesn't lead to any of the unfortunately fairly common hiker–biker confrontations.

There can be problems on a narrow trail when, approaching at a leisurely speed from one direction, is your walker, thinking for all the world that the only thing he's likely to encounter on the path is other walkers or wildlife, and rattling along at breakneck speed the other way is your mountain biker, often clad in full padded gear, intent on his adrenaline-fuelled descent. The outcome can vary but usually involves confrontational cursing if not actual bodily injury.

The need to share the trails and tracks in the region has led to necessary restrictions on mountain bikers during the summer months of July and August – see Restrictions below. These limits must be adhered to in the interests of future biking. Mountain bike itineraries are plentiful in Chamonix and it's no great loss to avoid the busy main valley trails when they are heaving with walkers, dogs, joggers and children. It just makes sense.

Since the last edition of this guidebook e-bikes have really taken off, both for road and mountain biking. While the routes described here remain good, there are now so many more options and it's worth checking on the Tourist Office websites to get the most recent and the most popular routes. Notably the St Gervais Tourist Office has produced an excellent leaflet detailing a number of routes for normal bikes and also routes for e-bikes.

*Mountain biking waymark*

## ROUTES

So where to go? 'Mountain bike' in French is *vélo tout terrain* (VTT). The local tourist offices have a special VTT booklet, which details the routes, along with maps. This is available in English and is free. It covers mountain biking routes from Servoz to Vallorcine. There is also a guidebook written in English called *Mountain Bike Chamonix Mont Blanc* by Tom Wilson-North. This describes various routes in detail and is a recommended purchase if you're going to spend several days biking.

## WAYMARKS AND GRADES

Mountain bike trails are signed with the symbol of a yellow triangle and two dots to look like an arrow. These arrows are on a coloured background and this denotes trail difficulty:

| Green: | easy |
| Blue: | moderate |
| Red: | difficult |
| Black: | experts |

Green routes can be done comfortably on hybrid bikes or basic mountain bikes, while blue rides will be more comfortable with front suspension. For harder, more technical routes and for big steep descents you'll need a full suspension bike with disc brakes – and for the black descents a strong nerve!

Sometimes you will see a yellow arrow on a white background. This just indicates a trail where mountain bikes are allowed.

Most mountain bike routes involve some road riding too. Take care – roads are dangerous.

## TIMES

Times are given here very reluctantly and are likely to be found to be incorrect for some riders. Unlike walking where there are norms, cyclists ascend and, in particular, descend at such different speeds that timings are very difficult to calculate. The distance of a ride and the altitude gain should give a good indication of how long it will take. If you find my times way out, then ignore them.

## BIKE RENTAL

There are quite a few bike shops in and around Chamonix. They all offer rental at competitive prices. Most shops offer several rental durations, from half-day to full day to multi-day. Rental usually includes helmets and also, for certain bikes, will include protective clothing too. In 2011

prices varied from around €20–€70 for a half-day and €30–€100 for the full day. For a list of bike shops see Appendix A.

## RESTRICTIONS

It is essential to note that there are important and enforced restrictions on mountain biking during July and August. Only the dedicated mountain bike trails in Chamonix are permitted to VTTs at that time. A list of authorised trails can be found in the free VTT guide available (in English) from tourist offices. Basically, in July and August you can only mountain bike on trails that are signed with VTT arrows. Biking is also strictly forbidden, year-round, in the Réserve des Aiguilles Rouges and other nature reserves.

Outside of July and August you can take your bike on every open lift

*Restrictions apply to mountain bikes throughout the area*

## MOUNTAIN BIKE CODE OF GOOD CONDUCT

- When on the road remember you are a regular road user.
- Wear a helmet.
- Slow down or get off when passing people on narrow trails. Equally, ring your bell when you approach people from behind.
- Ride at an appropriate speed for the nature of the terrain.
- Don't overestimate your ability.
- Respect '*privé*' signs, close gates, slow down when there are animals nearby, and take your litter home with you.
- Don't take shortcuts as these will quickly become eroded waterways which totally destroy the hillside.

If you want to get airtime or scare yourself silly go to a circuit set up for that – Le Dirt or one of the bike parks such as Bellevue at Les Houches.

except the Aiguille du Midi cable cars, the Montenvers Railway, the Tramway du Mont Blanc and the second stage of the Grands Montets cable car.

If mountain biking is something you want really want to concentrate on for several days it might be better to try to avoid the summer season. Early September is a better time as most of the lifts are still open, and there are fewer people.

However, don't let all these restrictions put you off; there are plenty of good trails to go at. Described in this chapter is a selection of routes from beginner valley biking to wild descent, but there are lots more to be found. Just look at the map, but do avoid single track and do be ready for hikers coming the other way.

Remember, mountain bikers are just one category of many using the trails in the Chamonix region.

### BIKES AND THE TRAIN

There are lots of possibilities for bike rides using the Chamonix valley Mont Blanc Express train (Martigny–Le Fayet) for the outward or return journey. Bikes are allowed but the number is limited to five bikes per train. So be aware that you could be refused access if there is no room for any more bikes. In this case just wait for the next train – or hop on your bike.

There is also now a bus service for mountain bikers with two routes, one from Chamonix to Vallorcine and one from Chamonix to Les Houches. There are several buses a day, and the service runs from early July to late August. Ask at the Tourist Office for more details.

# ROUTE 1

*Les Contamines: Truc Miage circuit*

| | |
|---|---|
| **Start** | Les Contamines-Montjoie, at La Frasse at the top of town |
| **Distance** | 7.9km |
| **Grade** | Blue |
| **Time** | 1hr 30min |
| **Altitude gain** | 450m |
| **Map** | IGN Top 25 3531 ET Saint-Gervais-les-Bains |

This circuit takes the rider to the edge of some marvellous glacial scenery, while staying on easy trails.

From **La Frasse** take the wide and steep forest track that goes up past Les Granges de la Frasse and into the forest. The steep start will leave you gasping for breath but things soon improve as the angle eases. At a junction go right on a pleasant track to emerge from the forest on a high plateau within sight of the **Chalets du Truc**.

Take the time to admire the breathtaking views of the Dômes de Miage and the Aiguille du Bionnassay, before picking up the single-track trail which zigzags down through slopes of alder to the wide open basin of the **Miage meadows**. A visit to the café here (across the stream in the meadows) would seem sensible, before returning across the stream to leave this idyllic location by the track which goes around the hillside on the left side of the stream – this is not the track to Champel, this one goes to La Gruvaz and Les Contamines. This track heads around the mountainside. After a descent a track goes off right to La Gruvaz, but don't take this, stay on the track to Les Contamines. At the next junction you'll regain the ascent route, which is followed back to La Frasse.

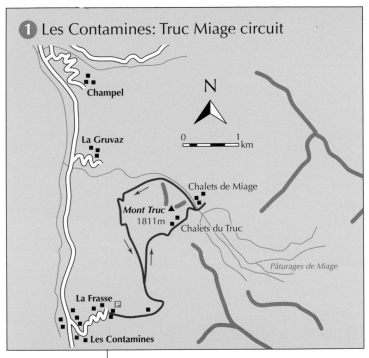

**① Les Contamines: Truc Miage circuit**

Champel

N

0    1 km

La Gruvaz

Chalets de Miage

*Mont Truc*
1811m

Chalets du Truc

Pâturages de Miage

La Frasse    P

Les Contamines

*The Bike Parks are set up for jumps and acrobatics – this one at Bellevue Les Houches also has a good view*

#  ROUTE 2
## *Saint-Gervais-les-Bains: Prarion circuit*

| | |
|---|---|
| **Start** | Saint-Gervais-les-Bains, at the car park for the cable car |
| **Distance** | 15km |
| **Grade** | Red except for the small part of the descent to Saint-Gervais, which should get black – but you could get off and walk. |
| **Time** | 4hr |
| **Altitude gain** | 1117m |
| **Map** | IGN Top 25 3531 ET Saint-Gervais-les-Bains |

This is a pleasant ride, a mix of small roads, tracks and trails, the high point of which is the Prarion Hotel Restaurant on the ridge separating Saint-Gervais from Les Houches. It is important to note that the descent back to Saint-Gervais is very steep near the end and gets slippery in wet weather. If you're unsure, it might be better to go back the way you've come, but it's still worth going as the Prarion ridge is such a superb viewpoint.

Head out of town on the main road to Les Contamines-Montjoie. After a few kilometres don't miss a turn left to **Bionnay**, then continue to **Bionnassay**. Go through the village and continue straight ahead up the jeep track, which is steep and rough in parts, to the **Col de Voza** (1653m). Be prepared for a visual feast when you get there!

Go left on the track towards **Prarion Hotel Restaurant**. Perhaps this might be the moment for a welcome drink, before back-tracking a little way to pick up the track that leads through **La Charme** and on down back to **Saint-Gervais**, rather too steeply towards the end. Remember, getting off is an option …

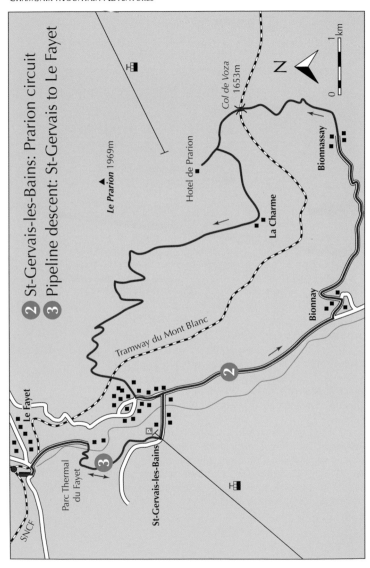

## 2 St-Gervais-les-Bains: Prarion circuit
## 3 Pipeline descent: St-Gervais to Le Fayet

Col de Voza 1653m

Bionnassay

Le Prarion 1969m

Hotel de Prarion

La Charme

Bionnay

Bionnay

Tramway du Mont Blanc

Le Fayet

Parc Thermal du Fayet

St-Gervais-les-Bains

SNCF

**ROUTE 3**

*Pipeline descent: Saint-Gervais to Le Fayet*

| | |
|---|---|
| **Start** | Saint-Gervais, at the car park for the cable car |
| **Distance** | 3.9km |
| **Grade** | Black |
| **Time** | 30min |
| **Altitude gain** | None |
| **Map** | IGN Top 25 3531 ET Saint-Gervais-les-Bains |

This unusual route provides challenging, fast and technical riding. The route in part follows an enormous water pipe and has some sections that will not be appreciated by those of a nervous disposition. The route requires experience on a mountain bike, skill and courage, and also a bike with full suspension and the gear to match. This one is *not* for beginners.

If you want to avoid a ride up the road to get back to Saint-Gervais you could leave a car at Le Fayet – the train station has a free car park – or if there are two or more in your group one person could get the public bus service back up to Saint-Gervais to collect the car.

Head down the Chemin de Fontaine Froide to a house with green shutters on the left where the road becomes a dirt track. Take this to a fork after a bench made of a plank on two stones. This right turn is easy to miss if you're enjoying the descent. Go right downhill and soon after turn right again at a sign 'Passerelle des thermes parc des thermes le Fayet'. The trail is narrow and leafy with some red-and-white paint flashes on trees. Watch out for a World War II big bomb crater in the middle of the trail – go round it, watching out for tree roots. At the next sign, 'Parc thermal du Fayet', go right down a steep descent to reach a big concrete water tank. There is a sign saying 'Tour d'eau 765m' where you go straight ahead towards the **Parc Thermal du Fayet**. This is where you follow the pipeline

*A rather wet descent of the Pipeline route (photo: Patricia Loffi)*

down with some fairly steep sections – watch out for some metal spikes on steps.

There is a green bench set back from the trail and just after this the route leaves the pipeline and descends in a series of steep hairpins, which are exposed with a cliff off to the side. Once this scary section is done you'll go over a bridge. Turn left down the path to the Le Fayet Thermal Park. Go out of the park gates and onto the main road. If you've left a car at Le Fayet, ride along the road to get there; otherwise, cycle up the road from Le Fayet back to St Gervais.

## 🚲 ROUTE 4
### Tour des Ayères

| | |
|---|---|
| **Start** | Park at Servoz near the Post Office or take the train to Servoz and head into town from the station |
| **Distance** | 13.5km |
| **Grade** | Red |
| **Time** | 2hr 30min |
| **Altitude gain** | 850m |
| **Map** | IGN Top 25 3530 ET Samoëns |

Ayères is a collection of summer hamlets situated under the imposing Rocher des Fiz and opposite the Mont Blanc massif, far above the Arve valley. The area is popular for hiking, biking and driving 4x4s. There is a well-situated café at Le Châtelet d'Ayères, which is open in the summer season. It's certainly worth taking some time among the Ayères hamlets to sit and enjoy those magnificent views.

This ride can be shortened by starting higher up, either at the Parking de la Côte or at Plaine Joux. But starting at Servoz gives the longest outing and provides lots of technical riding and great views.

It can also be lengthened by continuing on from Ayères to the Refuge Moëde d'Anterne, but to do this it is definitely more reasonable to start at Plaine Joux.

Although this location is idyllic, don't be surprised on summer weekends to see lots of four-wheel drive vehicles – the locals usually have these to access their chalets and they're allowed to drive right up. There is also regulated vehicle access to the Refuge Moëde d'Anterne.

Take the Route du Mont to the Fontaine du Mont, then at the first junction take the road on the left. Where the road flattens, take the track on the right (sign to Lac Vert), which brings you out below the Parking de la Côte. From here you can take the road or take the shortcuts, which cut the road twice, to reach **La Côte**. From the Parking de la Côte a 4x4 track goes up to **Lac Vert** and once there it's

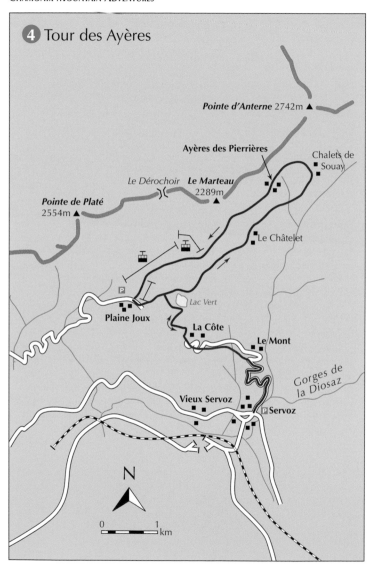

**4** Tour des Ayères

*Pointe d'Anterne* 2742m ▲

**Ayères des Pierrières**

Chalets de Souay

*Le Dérochoir*  **Le Marteau** 2289m ▲

*Pointe de Platé* 2554m ▲

Le Châtelet

Lac Vert

**Plaine Joux**

**La Côte**

**Le Mont**

Gorges de la Diosaz

**Vieux Servoz**

P **Servoz**

N

0  1 km

*Taking a break on the Tour des Ayères (photo: Patricia Loffi)*

definitely worth taking the time to look around – this is a popular spot and it's easy to see why.

The VTT route from Lac Vert is very clear, going in front of the restaurant. However, a better variation is to take the road on the left that goes up towards Plaine Joux and, after 150m or so, look for a track that crosses the road. Take this track right (there's a sign on the left saying 'Châtelet Ayères'), which leads above Lac Vert with some fantastic brief views of Mont Blanc in the background. At the first junction, go straight on where the track goes down on the right. Now you re-join the main VTT route which is marked with VTT arrows. It goes left alongside a water pipe.

A sign shows the black VTT route to the right but this way is technical and difficult with some steep sections. To the left is the red VTT route, which is easier and brings you out on the small road coming from Plaine Joux which goes all the way to **Châtelet d'Ayères**. This is the last proper parking area. From the parking, red VTT signs lead up a track to the **Chalets de Souay** then up to **Ayères des Pierrières**, the high point of the ride, and the panorama is magnificent.

Go between the houses, following the track which heads past Ayères des Rocs then to the top of the Plaine Joux ski pistes. These are followed, giving a fabulous descent to **Plaine Joux**, where you take the road down to Lac Vert and return by the ascent route.

 **ROUTE 5**

*Promenade de l'Arve*

| | |
|---|---|
| **Start** | Les Gaillands. Head out of Chamonix towards les Bossons; after a couple of kilometres you will see a hotel on the right called La Chaumière and soon after you'll find a large car park on the right, opposite a small lake. Park here. |
| **Distance** | 4km |
| **Grade** | Green |
| **Time** | 45min |
| **Altitude gain** | About 50m along the way |
| **Map** | IGN Top 25 3630 Chamonix Mont Blanc |

This is a lovely route, suitable for all the family, easy (by mountain bike standards), with super views. There are some uphill sections but they are short-lived and the terrain is smooth, so it's quite easy to pedal uphill. The ride starts at Les Gaillands, just outside Chamonix, home to Chamonix's most famous rock-climbing cliff, where generations of local alpinists have honed their skills. From here, you follow wide tracks all the way down to Les Houches where you can either turn around and come back or go and get the train back to Chamonix.

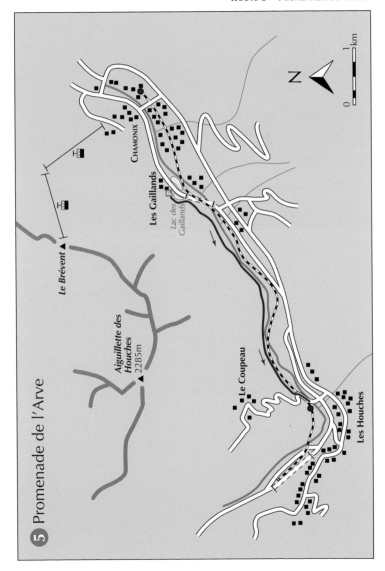

5 Promenade de l'Arve

203

*The Mont Blanc massif seen from the Arve*

Go to the far left upper corner of the car park and take the track signed Promenade de l'Arve, right next to the small lake (on the far side from the main road). In the autumn the start of the track is often obliterated by dead leaves, but it very soon becomes obvious and then it's plain sailing all the way. This route is popular with walkers, dogs, children and old people. Take care – but that said there really is room for everyone.

The way is signed when necessary and after about 25min you reach a barrier. Go around this onto the tarmac road where there are chalets and continue to a T-junction. This is basically the end of the Promenade and if you like you can just catch your breath and head right back.

Alternatively, to your left the road descends and goes over a big bridge. Just before this bridge a right turn takes you to Les Houches **train station** where you could hop on the train for the return to Chamonix. If cakes and cafés are calling, then you should continue over the bridge and cycle uphill for a few minutes to reach the small town of **Les Houches** itself, where those needs can be satisfied, before making your way back either on the train or by reversing the route.

**ROUTE 6**

*Petit Balcon Nord: Chamonix to Le Tour*

| | |
|---|---|
| **Start** | Ski de Fond building opposite the MBC café on the outskirts of Chamonix |
| **Distance** | 12.5km |
| **Grade** | Red/Black (The route is mainly graded red but the ascent to Lavancher gets black.) |
| **Time** | 2hr 15min |
| **Altitude gain** | 700m |
| **Map** | IGN Top 25 3630 Chamonix Mont Blanc |

The Petit Balcon Nord takes the north side of the Chamonix valley and provides good, interesting riding. This route is really one of the classic rides and consequently very popular.

Take the big track that parallels the main road on the left, heading north-east away from **Chamonix**. It is signed with red-and-blue VTT arrows. The track crosses a couple of small roads then soon leads under a bridge to the far side of the main road, past the Hotel de l'Arveyron. Take the dirt road on the left, not the tarmac road on the right, and go over a bridge and past the helicopter rescue headquarters (known locally as the **DZ**).

At the end of this area (known as the *Désert Blanc*) there is an optional extra which goes round on the right signed 'Norvège'. For this option go right over the wooden bridge and turn left to go up the long ascent to the top (known as *La Norvège*). The track continues and brings you back down to the wooden bridge. It seems that some VTT arrows are missing in this section but follow signs for Le Lavancher if in doubt.

The way onwards from the wooden bridge, with or without the Norvège option, is to go around the building at the end of the Désert Blanc on the right, to reach a track going up increasingly rocky and difficult trails into

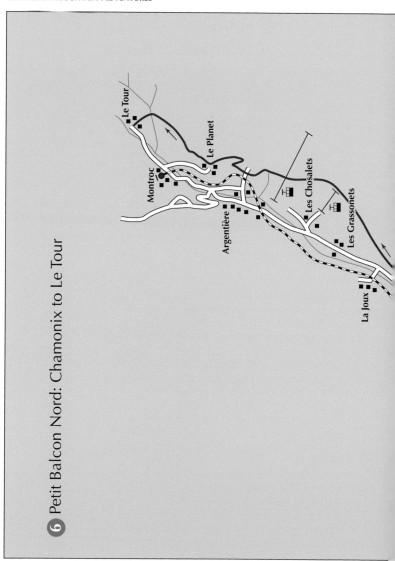

6 Petit Balcon Nord: Chamonix to Le Tour

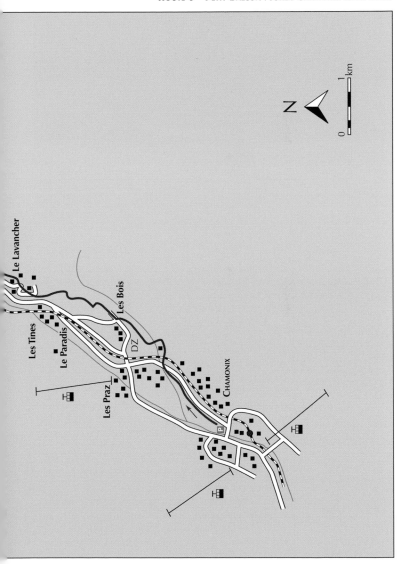

*Cycling towards the Désert Blanc at the start of Mountain Bike Route 6*

the forest, finally emerging on the road on the outskirts of **Lavancher** village. Turn left and enjoy a great road descent before braking suddenly at a Stop sign where you must turn right onto the Petit Balcon Nord, signed with red-and-blue VTT arrows.

Grassy terrain soon gives way to forest and one of the best parts of the route, over lots of tree roots, requiring good coordination and bike skills, with a short descent. After this excitement you'll reach a junction where you go right and up a steep and rough trail to the top of the drag-lifts at **Les Chosalets**. Another bumpy descent awaits, at the end of which is a useful sign 'slow down ralentir enfant'. Keep following the red VTT signs along more gentle terrain in the forest. The ascent is easy under the Grands Montets chairlift, to a wooden bridge, which you cross. Stay with the red arrows until you reach the path that goes up to **Le Planet** in steep zigzags, after which you'll probably want to stop for a breather and to enjoy fine views of the Chamonix valley – there is a handy flat area above Le Planet itself.

The Petit Balcon Nord continues all the way to the moraine under the Tour Glacier. Here you turn left and ride into **Le Tour**.

To return to Chamonix, the road from Le Tour leads down to Montroc where you can take the train back, or return via the main road through Argentière. Alternatively, from Montroc you could do Mountain Bike Route 7 along the Arve.

 # ROUTE 7

*Montroc to Chamonix along the Arve*

| | |
|---|---|
| **Start** | Take the train from Chamonix to Montroc station |
| **Distance** | 13.5km including the Col des Montets detour |
| **Grade** | Blue |
| **Time** | 1hr 30min |
| **Altitude gain** | 100m (+ undulations) |
| **Map** | IGN Top 25 3630 Chamonix Mont Blanc |

If done as described here, this route is mainly flat and in descent. Clearly it could be done in reverse for those who like uphill. It is generally fairly straightforward, with some narrower trails but mainly fairly wide tracks. There is a section that would be really easy if it weren't for frequent wooden bridges to negotiate, but these can be avoided if you're willing to splash through very shallow streams.

This route can be used as a return route for Mountain Biking, Route 6.

Get off the train and turn left. Go to the far end of the car park towards the train tunnel and you'll find a small path that goes over the tunnel and is signed to **Trè-le-Champ**. Follow this and go to Trè-le-Champ hamlet. Turn right along a big track that takes you out onto the main road. It's worth turning right here and following the road up to the **Col des Montets** at 1461m for some lovely views.

Come back down the road, which gives a superb descent right into and through **Argentière** village. Stay on the main road until you reach the big bend which swings left – on the right you'll see the Hotel des

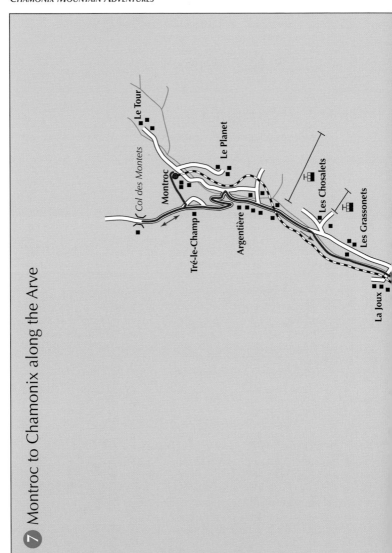

**7** Montroc to Chamonix along the Arve

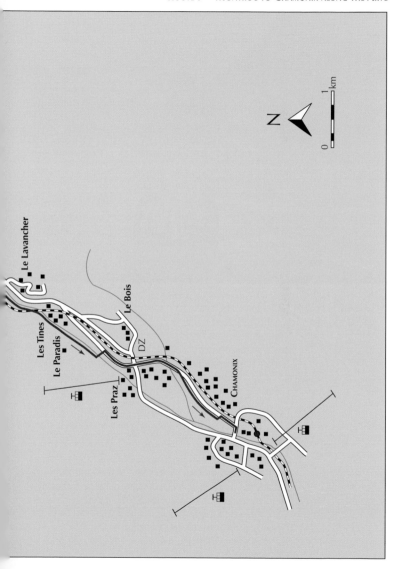

*Easy rolling cycling right next to the Arve*

Randonneurs. Leave the main road here and follow the wide track next to the river. Continue on this track, over the little bridges or streams. It takes you next to the railway at one point but keep going parallel to the river. The route is signed with red-and-blue VTT arrows, and there is a pretty steep descent just before you reach **Les Tines**. From here on the track can be very busy with families, dogs and children, not to mention other bikers. Take care and go slowly.

Just before **Le Paradis du Praz** you must stay on the left side of the stream that runs through this area. This is signed for bikes and bypasses Le Paradis, where there is a café and a kiddie's park. Once you re-join the main track you'll soon reach the golf course and then the Hotel Labrador car park. Head out onto the main road, go right up to the roundabout and straight on along the main road. Just after the bridge over the Arve there is a track off to the right into the woods, which leads to **Chamonix**.

**ROUTE 8**

*Col des Montets to the chocolate shops*

| | |
|---|---|
| **Start** | Col des Montets – the VTT bus service runs to here |
| **Distance** | 8km from the col to the frontier, then back from Le Buet |
| **Grade** | Green to the frontier; blue back up to the Col des Montets |
| **Time** | 1hr to the frontier; another 20min from Le Buet back up to the Col des Montets |
| **Altitude gain** | 120m |
| **Map** | IGN Top 25 3630 Chamonix Mont Blanc |

A chance to discover the Vallorcine valley and to cross an international frontier, with the additional attraction of buying very good chocolate in Le Châtelard. This route gives lovely views and terrain, sometimes in the open and sometimes in forest, and is another one for all the family. From the frontier take the train back to Le Buet, then it's a gentle ride back up to the Col des Montets.

From the bus stop at the **Col des Montets**, cycle down the little tarmac road next to the main road to where it comes out onto the main road, then head onto the big track going down towards Vallorcine. This leads pleasantly alongside the Eau Noire, Vallorcine's river. At a small bridge stay on the main trail, which rises slightly and takes you along through houses at Les Mayens des Biolles (opposite Le Buet station). After the houses, remain on the right of the railway and go down a grassy trail to a wooden bridge under the railway. Don't go under the railway; stay on the right side of it and follow the trail which moves away from the train line and goes down through meadows to **Vallorcine** itself, arriving at Vallorcine train station. Go left over the level crossing and through the big car park, out onto the main road.

Turn right and soon after turn left, just the other side of the Tourist Office, to take a smaller road towards

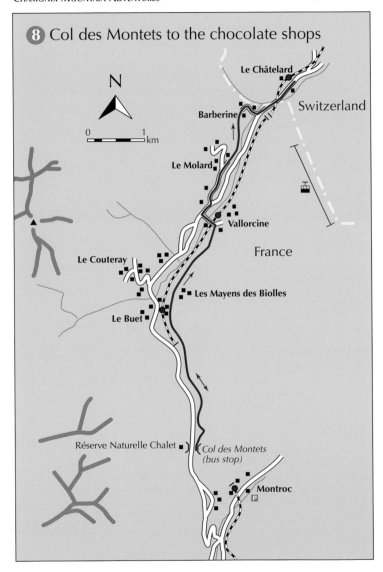

**8** Col des Montets to the chocolate shops

N

0      1 km

Le Châtelard

Switzerland

Barberine

Le Molard

Vallorcine

France

Le Couteray

Les Mayens des Biolles

Le Buet

Réserve Naturelle Chalet

Col des Montets
(bus stop)

Montroc

the church. Before the church stay right and go on and through the hamlet of **Le Molard**. A single-track path leads out of the hamlet into the forest and down to **Barberine**. Go down the road here and out onto the main road. Turn left to the Swiss border. Once past the customs buiding, there is a garage and chocolate shop on the right, and another further up the road on the left. There are also a couple of cafés on the left. The Châtelard Frontier railway station is on the left, before the garage on that side.

Take the train to Le Buet. Come out of the station and turn immediately right down a small road. Very quickly find a road on the right, which goes through a tunnel back to the houses at Les Mayens des Biolles. Retrace your outward route from here to the Col des Montets.

*Biking over the Col des Montets, take the time to enjoy the views which are stunning in both directions*

**ROUTE 9**

*Vallorcine–Col des Posettes–Le Tour–Montroc*

| | |
|---|---|
| **Start** | Drive (or take the train) to Vallorcine and park at the station |
| **Distance** | 10km |
| **Grade** | Red |
| **Time** | 2hr 30min |
| **Altitude gain** | 750m |
| **Map** | IGN Top 25 3630 Chamonix Mont Blanc |

While lifts can be used to avoid the uphill (or downhill!) this ride provides a good long ascent (750m) and descent for those old-school riders who still enjoy putting in the effort.

The Col des Posettes provides passage from the Vallorcine valley to the head of the Chamonix valley and as you approach the col you'll be rewarded with excellent views, firstly of the Aiguille Verte and the Droites then finally the whole of the Mont Blanc massif.

Go over the railway lines and turn left. Very soon a dirt track goes off right – this is the ski piste down to Vallorcine from the Col des Posettes in winter and provides a red VTT ascent in the summer. Follow this fairly gently graded track up through several long hairpin bends to reach a flat, where the Esserts chairlift will be seen off to the left. Continue up the track, over some drainage channels, to a right turn. Take this up to the top of the Vallorcine cable car. Just beyond you'll arrive at the **Col des Posettes** (1997m) and that superb vista.

The ski area of Le Tour has lots of VTT options. For the red route take the main track, which goes south-east to the top of Le Tour cable car (the bottom of the chairlift) at **Charamillon**. From there a big piste leads down steeply under the cable car all the way to **Le Tour**. For the return journey, ride down the road to the train station at Montroc, where you can take the train back to Vallorcine

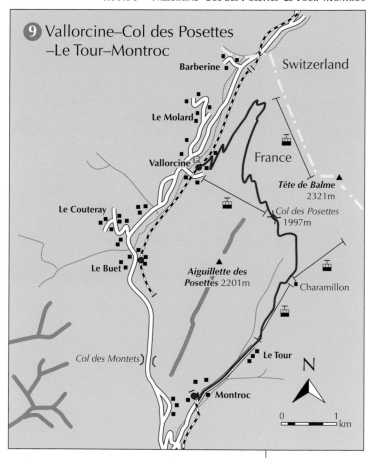

or to Chamonix. Alternatively you could ride over the Col des Montets back to the start, leaving the main road on the right just the other side of the col to join the Chemin des Diligences to Vallorcine.

**Note** A special VTT descent route exists from Charamillon to Le Tour. It is steep and exciting and I'm

*Taking a break at the Col des Posettes (photo: Marc Volorio)*

told provides the best way down for those equipped for such descents.

 **ROUTE 10**

*Vallorcine to Martigny*

| | |
|---|---|
| **Start** | Drive (or take the train) to Vallorcine train station |
| **Distance** | 18km |
| **Grade** | This route isn't officially graded. It's long so that probably makes it red, but nowhere is it very technical. The descent is fairly steep, but the ground isn't really rough or difficult. |
| **Time** | 2hr |
| **Altitude gain** | 350m |
| **Map** | Carte Nationale de la Suisse 1:50,000 5003 Mont Blanc Grand Combin |

A favourite, as you travel a long way from Vallorcine right down to the Swiss Rhône valley. This route could just as well be started in Chamonix, but let's be reasonable here, it is already quite a good length. The first part takes a nice trail alongside the railway to reach Switzerland, then joins the main road briefly before heading up the minor road to Finhaut village. From here it picks up the Chemin des Diligences, which is the old carriage way that came from Martigny to Chamonix. This track is a really great bike ride, partly because it's varied and interesting, and also because it's largely downhill and leads all the way down to the train station at Vernayaz near Martigny, from where you can take the train back to Vallorcine. All in all, a grand day out, but be sure to take your passport.

From **Vallorcine** train station cycle over the level crossing and turn left on a wide piste. Stay on this and after a bridge on the left it becomes a smaller trail and goes all the way down the valley alongside the railway line. There are a couple of small dips and rises along the way but don't exit until you reach the bottom, where the train goes into a tunnel and the trail goes over the top and descends very steeply – be careful not to slide off the edge as the tree roots are often slippery. A short flight of wooden steps leads to the road.

Go out onto the main road and through the customs post, then continue along the main road for a kilometre or so, past a first turning on the left to **Le Châtelard**, to a second large turning which is signed to **Finhaut**. Take this road, which goes down, under a bridge, and up past a road going off right to the village. Stay on the main road, which goes onwards to Emosson.

You're looking for a track going off right, just after a big bend round to the left, opposite a small road which comes up on the left from the village. There is a fountain, an information board for the Espace Mont Blanc, and a signpost for Les Marecottes and Salvan.

This track is the Chemin des Diligences and has a Swiss red bike sign. It goes into the forest, flat at first, then descends in tight hairpins to come out at **Le Tretien**,

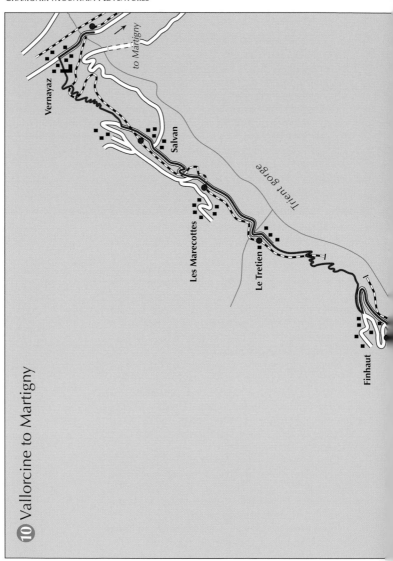

10 Vallorcine to Martigny

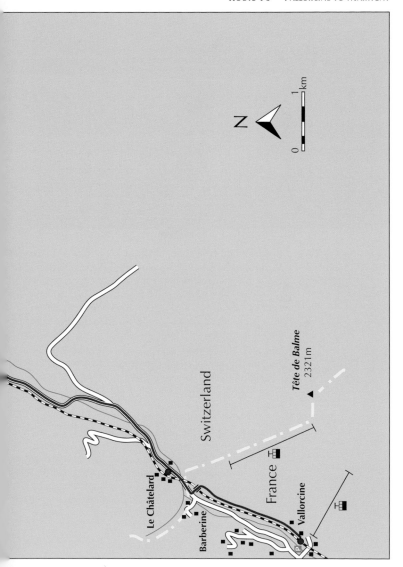

*Heading along the Chemin des Diligences*

a small hamlet. A minor road joins Le Tretien to **Les Marecottes**, which is a charming little village with a zoo and a swimming pool. It's on the railway line so escape is possible here. At a junction after the zoo, go left then right to **Salvan** and once you've descended into Salvan village go left at a right-hand bend on a smaller road which passes the Post Office, heading to Les Granges. Stay on this small road, passing under the railway bridge and, immediately after, the tarmac road goes left and the Chemin des Diligences resumes as a dirt track. There is a red barrier, usually open, a red VTT sign and yellow footpath signs.

Get ready for another good descent, again with lots of tight zigzags, all the way down to the valley. The trail emerges at an electricity station in the town of **Vernayaz**. Go right on the main road and you'll find the Vernayaz railway station or you can continue on the road into Martigny. If you do this you'll go past a couple of roundabouts. One of them features a very fine minotaur – left here leads to the train station, right to the main street and lots of welcome outdoor cafés.

Getting airtime

Chamonix, Les Houches, Argentière, Vallorcine and Le Tour all offer exciting mountain biking options for those who are not interested in toiling uphill. These areas are well documented in the local VTT leaflet, so here's just a brief outline of what's available for adrenaline junkies.

**St Gervais le Fayet**

The Charlotte la Marmotte bike park provides some really fun mountain biking at all levels. This park is high up on the slopes of Mont Arbois, accessed by cable car from St Gervais. The views are magnificent and the biking is well thought out. 1.5kms may seem short but there's enough for a great family outing.

Equally entertaining is the Wizz descent which could easily be combined with a session at the Charlotte bike park. This 5km descent leads from the top of the cable car to the middle station of the lift system and has been specially designed for mountain bikers who are still learning to deal with the challenges of downhill. It features built-up bends, wooden bridges and some optional jumps. From the mid station it's possible to follow another signed descent into town.

*Many mountain bike trails lead to fabulous belvederes*

### Bellevue Mountain Bike Park, Les Houches

From the top of the Bellevue lift at Les Houches the Bike Park is easy to find. There are lots of features for budding mountain bike acrobats, such as see-saws, drop-offs and jumps. There is also a Classic Piste, which is a downhill track with 600m of vertical drop.

### Grand Montets (Lognan)

From the Lognan cable car there are a couple of descents, notably the main ski piste.

### Vallorcine

The ski piste through the forest provides a great descent and is wide enough for hikers too. A good place for a blast.

*On a trail near Le Lavancher, above the valley*

### Le Tour

This village also boasts a VTT piste that starts at the top of the cable car and descends in a fabulous series of dips and jumps all the way to the car park.

# 4 ROAD BIKING

*Chamonix is a great place to road bike if you like hills and great scenery*

Road biking in the Alps is a dream for many cyclists and it's certainly worth taking your road bike to Chamonix, or hiring one while there. From Chamonix you can feasibly bike several of the iconic alpine passes, notably the Col de la Colombière and the Col des Aravis, both of which have regularly featured on the Tour du France circuit. Much nearer to Chamonix though there are plenty of good rides you can do directly from your Chamonix base.

The roads in the Alps are rarely flat, but the climbs are generally not as steep as those found in the UK. However, the climbs go on for much longer – 1000m of ascent is not uncommon and when you calculate that ascent at an average of 6% the climb will be 17km long!

In addition, cycling on French roads is different to cycling in the UK. French drivers are generally fairly courteous to cyclists but there are rules of the road in France that differ from those in the UK.

The obvious one is that in France you ride on the right.

There is an old but still valid rule that traffic gives way to vehicles coming from the right. If a road comes in from the right and has no 'give way' sign or stop line, then the vehicle coming from the right has priority, even if this is a minor road joining a major highway. Old drivers particularly are very fond of this rule and don't even look to see if anything is coming from their left.

Roundabouts seem to present a challenge to many French drivers. They sometimes stop halfway around to allow a vehicle in, they rarely indicate, or they indicate right when they are going straight on. Take great care!

The mountain roads provide extra challenges. A fast road biker will descend faster than many cars but overtaking on a fast descent can be hazardous. Moreover, drivers on such windy roads often cut corners so overtaking can be very dangerous. Cold snowy winters play havoc with the road surfaces and there are often big potholes on the mountain roads, or unexpected bumps and dips where temperature variations cause the surface below to contract.

## GEAR

- Your bike should be equipped with lights as there are often tunnels on mountain roads. While lights in the daytime are not a legal requirement in France, in a dark tunnel they would seem a prudent choice. At night, lights on bikes are required by law.
- In France all bikes are supposed to be equipped with a bell. I have never heard of this being enforced … but it's a useful addition to your ride.
- Helmet – not negotiable.

- It can be really hot in the alpine valleys – 40°C is not that uncommon in mid-summer down at 400m. The temperature is likely to drop dramatically from the valley to the high passes at 1500m so layers are essential. The descents are also often very cold and since they are so long it's sometimes impossible to warm up.
- A mobile phone is essential just in case.
- Full repair kit.
- An identity card or wristband is a good idea just in case the worst happens. You should have your passport with you anyway, especially if you're going to cross into Switzerland.

## TIMES

No times are given here for rides. Unlike walking where there are norms, cyclists ascend and descend at such different speeds that timings would be of little use. The distance of a ride and the altitude gain should give a good indication of how long it will take.

## MAPS

These routes require road maps and the descriptions in this chapter should enable easy location of the actual objectives and then the roads. For the main cols the average incline is given.

# ROUTE 1
*Chamonix to Sallanches*

| | |
|---|---|
| **Start** | Les Gaillands, just outside Chamonix |
| **Finish** | Outskirts of Sallanches 550m |
| **Distance** | 28kms |
| **Altitude gain** | About 100m from Les Houches to Vaudagne and a few short rises along the back road from Servoz, but essentially it's downhill all the way. |

Bikes are not allowed on the Route Blanche once outside Chamonix and who would want to ride this busy road anyway, with trucks hammering past. It's possible to have an enjoyable ride down to Sallanches on minor roads.

Start from **Les Gaillands**, or cycle out of town as far as there, and continue through Les Bossons and into **Les Houches**. Cycle through Les Houches but don't go out onto the main road. Follow the smaller road towards **Les Chavants** then stay right rather going up to Les Chavants, going straight ahead along a small and rough road to the hamlet of **Vaudagne**. Beware, this is potential puncture terrain: ride gently to Vaudagne as parts of the road are in a poor state. Follow this narrow, bendy road out of Vaudagne, towards Le Fayet and Sallanches. This takes you to a crossing under the N205, and over the other side of the Arve valley, to pick up the road into **Servoz**.

Go through Servoz and follow the signs to **Passy**. This attractive back road is great for cycling, and also has magnificent views of Mont Blanc. In Passy there is a roundabout (and a water fountain) and the road down to Sallanches is signposted straight ahead. Once down in the valley there are intermittent cycling lanes along the busier road into **Sallanches**. If you want to take the train back, either pick it up at Sallanches or more logically cycle back to Le Fayet and take the Mont Blanc Express up to Chamonix.

*Great views from the road between Servoz and Passy*

## ROUTE 2
*Col des Montets*

| | |
|---|---|
| **Start** | Chamonix |
| **Finish** | Col des Montets 1461m |
| **Distance** | 11.7km |
| **Average incline** | 3.3% |
| **Altitude gain** | 410m |

This pass sees lots of cyclists and is in itself a good aim for recreational cyclists. It has also had its moments of glory, being included on the Tour de France six times so far, the most recent being 1977.

Cycle north out of the town towards Switzerland. The average incline on the way up is 3.3% and **Col des Montets** is the first col that you come to.

If you descend the other side you can go all the way down to the Swiss border (**Le Châtelard**) then either hop on the train back to Chamonix or cycle back – 8.2km back to the col, with an average ascent of 4.6%.

 ## ROUTE 3
*Emosson Lake*

| | |
|---|---|
| **Start** | Chamonix |
| **Finish** | Emosson Lake 1965m |
| **Distance** | 32km one way |
| **Altitude gain** | 1280m total |

The Emosson Lake is a splendid objective for a bike ride as the road is well graded, the ascent fairly relentless and the views from the lake are spectacular and unusual.

Go over the **Col des Montets** to **Vallorcine** (or take the train from Chamonix and start in Vallorcine). Continue down the road to the Swiss frontier at **Le Châtelard** and continue for a couple of kilometres to a wide road on the left which goes up to **Finhaut** village. Instead of actually going into the village stay on the road that goes above the houses and continues in several long zigzags up to **Emosson Lake**. You could return by bike all the way to Chamonix, or get on the train at Le Châtelard.

 ## ROUTE 4
*Col de la Forclaz*

| | |
|---|---|
| **Start** | Martigny |
| **Finish** | Col de la Forclaz 1527m |
| **Distance** | 13km |
| **Average incline** | 9% |
| **Altitude gain** | 1000m |

This pass is well known to anyone who's driven out from Chamonix to Switzerland. It is the wide open pass which takes you down into the huge flat Rhône valley and the Valais canton and the views from the pass and during the descent to Martigny are exceptional. As well as the close-up views of the vineyards, the castle and the Roman amphitheatre in Martigny, you can see all the way along the Rhône valley to the shapely peak of the Bietschhorn in the Bernese Oberland. The Col de la Forclaz is also very popular with motorbikers who generally cruise up there and take a break at the restaurant at the top – much appreciated by thirsty cyclists too.

*The road from Martigny to the Col de la Forclaz gives wonderful views along the Swiss Rhône Valley (here filled with a sea of cloud) all the way to the Bernese Oberland*

This pass can of course be tackled directly from Chamonix via the Col des Montets, or for an easier option, take the train to Vallorcine and continue from there. However, the real challenge of the Col de la Forclaz is to bike it from Martigny. Take the train to Martigny then come back over the pass and onwards to Chamonix. Or just do an up and down from Martigny – the descent is a dream! The average incline on the way up from Martigny is 9%.

# 🚴 RIDES OUTSIDE OF THE CHAMONIX VALLEY

## Col de Pierre Carrée 1843m

This is the pass that gives access to the resort of Flaine, situated way above Sallanches on the east side of the Arve valley. The ride in its entirety (21.1km) starts at Balme, which is down in the valley at 500m, and goes all the way to the col in a massive 1500m climb. However, it is perfectly acceptable to start higher up, either at Araches (950m) or Les Carroz (1100m) to make a more reasonable ascent of 700–800m. The whole ride benefits from wide roads which makes riding more pleasant and hopefully safer.

This is a great climb, wherever you start, with an average slope of 6.4%, reaching a maximum of 8.4%.

The first part, as far as Les Carroz, is fairly irregular with steep sections interspersed with flatter parts. The road goes past some fine climbing cliffs at first, then the views open up to the Aravis and the characteristic rocky Pointe Percée summit.

From Les Carroz there is a short descent, then the ascent continues steadily all the way to the col, where there is a military post. Views are superb, with the Aravis peaks above the Arve valley far below.

*The cycle route along the Rhône Martigny–Sion–Martigny is a joy: car-free, fairly flat and scenic*

## Col de la Colombière 1613m and Col des Aravis 1486m

Both of these cols are eminently accessible by driving down to the Arve valley and heading off from there. The Col de la Colombière 1613m provides a passage between the Grand Bornand and the Reposoir valleys. Along with the Col des Aravis these two passes traverse the Aravis range and provide great bike rides for those with the requisite legs and lungs. Both are quite steep with maximum grades of 10% and 11%. They are also classic Tour de France ascents.

## Along the Rhône from Martigny

If you park in Martigny town you'll soon find little red cycling signs showing the way out and then along narrow tarmac roads beside the Rhône river. You can do a well signed route from Martigny to Sion, which is just short of 30km each way, almost totally flat and largely car-free. Sounds a dream? Well it is, but expect strong winds most days.

## Sallanches to Servoz

If you go down to the Arve valley you can park at Sallanches and head out along the back road to Passy and then onwards to Servoz. The road from Passy to Servoz is really pretty and surprisingly undulating. (See Route 1.)

## Passy to the Plateau d'Assy

This gently rising road takes you in graceful hairpins up to the village of Plateau d'Assy for superlative views of the Mont Blanc massif.

## Cluses to Sixt Fer à Cheval

This is a great ride of around 25km to Sixt itself then another 6km to the end of the road and the spectacular cirque of the Fer à Cheval. It's a bit different to the other rides described as there is a significant distance of rolling or flat terrain, after the initial climb out of Cluses. This gives you the chance to enjoy the scenery and makes a change from the habitual relentless grind of road biking in the Alps.

## Léman to Mont Blanc

This signed road route will take the cyclist from Lac Léman (Lake Geneva) all the way to Chamonix, via 80km of back roads. It is still being prepared but should be a great ride when it's finished. The section through Chamonix is already signed up for about 8km.

There are also lots of other road biking options and a look at the map will allow you to make up your own routes.

# 5 ROCK CLIMBING AND BOULDERING

*Climbers topping out on the Index, with the Aiguille Verte behind*

## ROCK CLIMBING

Chamonix is best known for its soaring granite faces and spiky rocky ridges, but there is also a wealth of valley climbing on crags close to the road with routes of all grades. These valley crags have historically been the training ground of alpinists honing their skills for ascents in the high mountains. Cliffs such as Les Gaillands have a real history attached to them, and for decades the elite climbers of the day would establish routes on these cliffs which were regarded as test-pieces, but were nevertheless just a prelude to what they were going to do up on the mountain faces. Nowadays many climbers would be horrified by the idea of hiking uphill for hours to reach the cliff and these crags provide fun playgrounds for passionate rock-jocks as well as those more newly acquainted with the sport.

Featured here are the best crags with routes of a moderate standard, places to go for a pleasant day on the rock, with great mountain views and beautiful climbs. For those keen to push their grades, there are plenty of harder routes on almost all the crags featured here Only a selection of routes are covered because at least three comprehensive guidebooks are available in English to the Chamonix crags. A quick glance through these guides will show that anyone coming to Chamonix exclusively for rock climbing will find more than enough go at, from one-pitch routes to multi-pitch.

- *Crag Climbing in Chamonix* by François Burnier and Dominique Potard. This is the basic valley climbing guide, reproduced every couple of years but with little editing. It will get you to the crags and then you might get confused, but where the route names are written at the bottom you'll probably figure it out. A little patience can be required.

- *The Aiguilles Rouges 1* by Michel Piola. This guide covers the crags in the Aiguilles Rouges from the Index to Les Chéserys. These are generally higher crags that require some walking approach but using the Flégère and Index lifts these approaches are not excessive. A second volume is planned which will cover the rest of the area and beyond, above the Vallorcine valley. However, due to the relatively high altitude and the required lift access these routes are really only feasible when the lifts are running. Some routes can be done in winter if skis are used for access and if it's very sunny, but generally this is regarded as a high-summer climbing area.

- *Les classiques et les nouveaux spots de Barberine Giétroz* by Jon de Montjoye. This small but

*Something for everyone at Les Gaillands*

comprehensive guide includes the Barberine slabs mentioned here, but also has all the other cliffs above and around these slabs. The Barberine Giétroz area is the motherlode for climbers looking for perfect rock, incredibly varied climbing and fantastic location. In addition, these crags can be climbed more or less year-round and require a maximum of 30min to access. The whole area is a maze, with multi-pitch gems nestling in among fine one-pitch routes, many of which get the sun the whole day as well as benefitting from the micro-climate of Giétroz.

**Climbing gear**

All the routes described here are equipped with bolts, so additional gear is not usually needed. (The exception to this is the Index, where a few nuts/friends are useful). However, always bear in mind that fixed gear is not infallible – use your own judgement when trusting an anchor.

Rope requirements vary from 50m to 80m to single to double ropes. Rope length is noted for each crag. Many of these accessible cliffs are popular in the summer season so care should be taken when climbing above other people, or indeed when there are other climbers above you. Wearing a helmet is a very wise move.

## BOULDERING

Those climbers who really want to keep it simple or who are keen to get really strong tend to be most attracted

*Climbing on Le Transat at the Col des Montets*

to bouldering. Over the past decade bouldering has become increasingly popular in the Chamonix region, as it has in most climbing areas worldwide. There are several bouldering sites in the Chamonix valley itself, and others just outside, and each year sees new areas developed. Keep your eyes open when driving from Chamonix to Vallorcine and you're sure to see roadside boulders adorned with chalk. Again, this is a sport that can be enjoyed for a good part of the year here – in fact spring and autumn tend to be preferable to summer when the temperatures can be a little high. October is often a beautiful month in the Alps and the crisp cold air gives the best friction on the boulder problems, so 'pad people' abound.

Bouldering is also popular as an after-work workout and doesn't require a partner – it's generally more fun not to be alone but the chances are you'll meet someone else anyway.

The classic Pierre d'Orthaz just outside Chamonix was the boulder all visiting climbers had heard of in the 1970s and it was certainly the place to be seen at that time. While still climbed on it has been somewhat eclipsed by the wealth of sites on offer these days.

The main site in the Chamonix valley, at the Col des Montets, is described here. It features problems of all grades in a beautiful setting. Sun and shade can be found, but for those cranking it out on the technical problems, late afternoon/evening seems to give the best conditions. The boulders at the col have been popular for many years and generations of climbers have fine-tuned their skills in this magnificent setting.

In the last few years several other sites have been developed

*Ibex showing us how to boulder*

*Cruising the traverse on Le Transat (photo: Marc Volorio)*

as bouldering becomes more and more a mainstream mountain sport. These other sites within the area are described only briefly because a full topo guide exists for these sites: *Les Blocs autour de Chamonix* by Romain Desgranges and Fabrice Judenne.

Hiking around the valley you'll probably spot boulders here and there that are obviously climbed on but some of them remain local secrets – it's easy to have a go and figure out existing problems as well as maybe inventing new ones. In the end,

bouldering is the simplest of sports – just pick a rock and see if there are any holds that you can use.

## Bouldering gear

Bouldering is as simple as it gets; for the purists this is climbing as it should be. However, even falling just a metre backwards can have terrible consequences so a pad of some sort is now regarded as essential. If you have a friend to spot you as well that's even better. Apart from that, just climbing shoes and a chalk bag should do it.

# ROCK CLIMBING

 AREA 1

*Les Gaillands*

| | |
|---|---|
| **Start** | Les Gaillands car park |
| **Guidebook** | *Crag Climbing in Chamonix* by François Burnier and Dominique Potard |
| **Access** | The cliffs are situated about 2km from the centre of Chamonix. Take the road out of town that is signposted 'Les Gaillands' and park at the cliffs, opposite a lake. There is always some sort of climbing demonstration on around 14 or 15 August, which is the Fête des Guides in Chamonix, and access to the main part of Les Gaillands will be limited at this time. |
| **Rope required** | Some routes require an 80m, or double 50m, but for others a single 60m will suffice. See descriptions. |

This is *the* Chamonix valley crag, traditional training ground for aspirant alpinists since the 1930s. It still draws the crowds and it's extremely rare to see this crag empty even on days when most people wouldn't consider climbing. There are several sectors to this crag and included here are the sectors in the sunny meadow where you park – Grand Gailland on the left, Les Monchus next to it, L'Echelle to the right and then Petit Gailland on the far right.

Expect the crag to be very busy on any sunny day in the holidays, and also on Wednesday afternoons and weekends. Even when it's too cold to climb elsewhere in the valley, it might be warm enough here, so long as the sun is out. However, beware – there can be a significant avalanche risk in winter from the huge slopes above. The sun leaves the Grand Gailland early afternoon but stays on the rest of the crag all day. The crags have largely been equipped, and continue to be maintained, by the Compagnie des Guides. Expect to find some of the traditional grades on the main cliffs described here somewhat severe. If you have an innate fear of small children then best avoid this place – at least half of the people present on any day will almost certainly be less than 1m tall.

Grand Gailland     Les Monchus     L'Echelle     Petit Gailland

At first sight it all seems quite confusing, and in fact might continue to do so as the local Chamonix guidebook is incomplete and inaccurate. However, the routes described below are good and can be found easily.

Locate the ladder more or less in the centre of the crags. To the right of this is the L'Echelle sector. This sector ends at a chimney and then right again is the Petit Gailland. Left of the ladder is a sector that is lower in height; this is Les Monchus. The left side of this sector is defined by a deep chimney and the sector left of this is Grand Gailland.

### Grand Gailland

Grand Gailland is all quite confusing as several routes start well up the crag so you have to climb up there first. The lower part of this crag has lots of first pitches, with loads of bolts and belays so it's probably simplest to just pick one. Just to give some pointers, locate the obvious pillar at the right-hand end of the crag, which has a good 6a up it. Left of this is a line of brown bolts, then left again a line of silver bolts. These silver bolts give a nice

grade 5 pitch to some first belays, then there is a continuation groove at around 4c to reach the second belay ledge. It's 40m to this point.

From the higher ledge there are quite a few routes. If you belay over on the right you'll see an obvious light-coloured groove above. This is 'Dièdre Rouge' (although it's not red) and is a good 6a, 20m (route number 6 in the guidebook). A pillar separates it from the next groove on the left, which is 4b and again 20m (number 8 in the guidebook). Then at the far left-hand end of the ledge system (change belays) there is a classic groove 'Diédre Gris', which is also 20m, grade 4c and excellent (route number 12 in the guidebook). To be sure of getting down safely, it's best to use an 80m single or double ropes. You can lower off these upper pitches, then descend by abseiling down to the first belays then down again from there.

### Les Monchus

Les Monchus has lots of easier routes, in the 3–4 grade, which are very popular with families. There are no protection points so the only way to climb here is for someone to climb up unprotected to set up a top rope. There are belays at various intervals, but at 60m rope will suffice, just stop at a belay before you reach the halfway mark on the rope. No topo is provided for this part of the crag as it's simply a matter of heading up and placing a top rope.

## L'Echelle
L' Echelle just to the right of the long ladder, has some good routes. Two routes take the obvious bulge at the left-hand end: the left route is 6a+ and the right-hand route 5c+ (routes 1 and 2 in the guidebook). Then just to the right are several fine pitches around grade 5. A rope of 60m is plenty to lower off these routes.

## Petit Gailland
At the right side of the cliffs the ground at the base of the crag rises up and there is a pillar at the base of the crag, which is bolted. To the right and behind this is the start of two routes. The start is in common for both. Go up behind

Climbing at Les Gaillands, on the upper part of Le Grand Gailland

Petit Gailland

5b La Plaque Rouge

Variante 5c

the pillar and climb past two bolts. (There is a rogue bolt in a blank wall to the right at the start – ignore this.)

The route splits after two bolts. The right-hand line is 5b ('Plaque Rouge' in the guidebook – despite the fact that it's the other line that climbs the red slab) and the left takes the fine red slab ('Variante' in the guidebook) and is 5c. They go to the same anchor. These routes are long and you should either take double ropes and abseil down or use an 80m.

 **AREA 2**

*The Index*

| | |
|---|---|
| **Start** | Les Praz cable car |
| **Guidebook** | *The Aiguilles Rouges 1* by Michel Piola |
| **Access** | Take the cable car to La Flégère then the Index chairlift. From the top of the chairlift head up left to gain the grassy terrace that runs across the east face of the Index and follow this almost to its left extremity, to rope up under a red chimney (15min) |
| **Rope required** | Double 50m ropes |

The Index is a striking finger of rock right next to the Index chairlift above the Flégère cable car. It is so close to the lift that it can be regarded as a crag rather than an alpine climb, and it certainly has the quickest and easiest approach of any cliff in the Aiguilles Rouges. The most popular route up the Index takes the SE ridge and is a classic Chamonix climb, a collector's item, so don't expect to be alone …! It was first climbed in 1913, so the rock is clean and rather polished and the itinerary easy to follow. With its short approach, four pitches, one abseil and quick descent it can be envisaged as a half-day route.

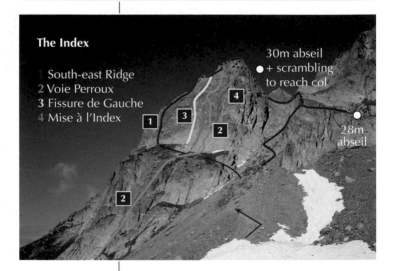

**The Index**

30m abseil + scrambling to reach col

1 South-east Ridge
2 Voie Perroux
3 Fissure de Gauche
4 Mise à l'Index

28m abseil

### The Index by the SE ridge

- Pitch 1: Climb the chimney and smooth slab 4c
- Pitch 2: Follow twin cracks 4a
- Pitch 3: Follow the arête 4b
- Pitch 4: Climb on the left side of the ridge then regain the ridge to climb a steep section of red rock. Continue on the right side and climb a short chimney then cross to the left side again to gain the summit. 4b.

To descend from the summit, scramble down on the left side to an abseil point on a ledge on the arête. From here climb up 20m on the opposite side of the col to join an easy ridge. Descend this and then there are two possibilities. Either look for a rocky ramp leading down into the couloir on the right or continue down further and slightly left to find an abseil point. A 28m abseil leads to the screes below.

**Other routes**
There are several other routes on the index itself: Voie Perroux, Fissure de Gauche and Mise à l'Index are all in the grade 5/6a range (see topo).

Nearby, other classic routes abound. Two to mention are on the nearby Contrefort de l'Aiguille de la Glière, which is just down and right of the Index, accessed by a 28m abseil. Mani Puliti (6 pitches 5b+) and Nez rouge (6 pitches 5b) have become classics since they were equipped in the late 1990s. See Piola's guidebook for full details.

# AREA 3
*La Joux*

<table>
<tr><td>**Start**</td><td>Park at La Joux train station</td></tr>
<tr><td>**Guidebook**</td><td>*Crag Climbing in Chamonix* by François Burnier and Dominique Potard</td></tr>
<tr><td>**Access**</td><td>From Chamonix take the main road towards Argentière and just after the paravalanche tunnel, 2km before Argentière, turn left on the Route de la Joux and drive up to the station car park. If coming by train, be aware that this stop is a request stop. Walk across the railway line through a couple of red-and-white gates, then turn right away from the village. There are signs to the cliff, which is referred to as Plaque Bellin, and it is the Petit Balcon Sud path. After a big clearing the path goes into the forest, and is signed all the way to the crag (10min).</td></tr>
</table>

**Rope required**    For the Plaque Bellin double 50m ropes; for the Gros Caillou and Le Diamant a single 60m rope.

This traditional training ground has been reinstated as new routes have been equipped and old routes re-equipped. It's now a very popular and pleasant spot right next to a clear flowing stream, enjoying lovely views.

Locate the Plaque Bellin on the far left – the trail is a little overgrown but just below the crag is a sign telling you to carry out your rubbish. This pillar gives at least two really good two-pitch routes of grade 4/5. The only downside is reaching the base of the routes. This is generally done via a short traverse which when free-climbed is 6b+ but which has been equipped for aiding. So pull on the bolts, get installed on the wall, then enjoy the routes.

Over to the right is the Gros Caillou, a big boulder that has numerous moderate routes on it. To the right again is a nice slab, Le Diamant, with several routes of moderate grade, two of which are shown on the topo at the far right end.

# AREA 4
*Les Chéserys*

| | |
|---|---|
| **Start** | Opposite Tré-le-Champ, about 500m before the col |
| **Guidebook** | *The Aiguilles Rouges 1* by Michel Piola |
| **Access** | From Chamonix head up the road towards the Col des Montets. Park on the left opposite Tré-le-Champ. Follow the trail towards Lac Blanc for about an hour to the base of the slabs. There is a slab on the trail with some log steps and a small path goes off right here to lead to the base of the cliffs. It arrives right under the Voie de l' EMHM on the central sector. |
| **Rope required** | Double 50m ropes |

Beautiful gneiss slabs high above the valley, with lots of moderate slab climbs. Multi-pitch. (In his guide Piola spells the crag 'Chézerys').

The classic Voie Blanche route is on the far end of the left-hand sector, just right of a steep gully. Voie Blanche is a great old classic but there are now various newer and perhaps better routes equipped on the same piece of rock – notably Une Père Noël pour Lucy and Désert de Samba. However, these are slightly harder. Sticking to the classic moderates, the others to go for are the Voie de l'EMHM and the Voie Bleue, both on the central sector. All three classic routes are about the same grade of 5c maximum (see topos).

Descent is by abseil down the routes.

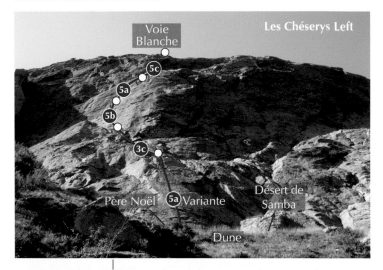

Les Chéserys Left

Voie Blanche
5c
5a
5b
3c
Père Noël
5a Variante
Désert de Samba
Dune

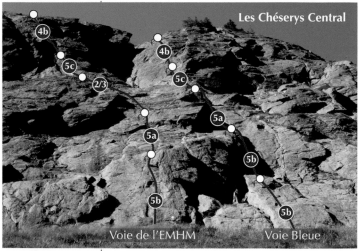

Les Chéserys Central

4b
4b
5c
5c
2/3
5a
5a
5b
5b
5b
Voie de l'EMHM
Voie Bleue

# 🛐 AREA 5
*Aiguillette d'Argentière*

| | |
|---|---|
| **Start** | Opposite Tré-le-Champ, about 500m before the col |
| **Guidebook** | *The Aiguilles Rouges 1* by Michel Piola |
| **Access** | As for the Chéserys slabs, further along the trail just before the ladders which form the continuation of the Lac Blanc trail (1hr 15min). |
| **Rope required** | 60m single or double 50m ropes |

A striking needle of rock, the Aiguillette d'Argentière gives some unusual routes and can be combined with a visit to the Chéserys slabs. Multi-pitch.

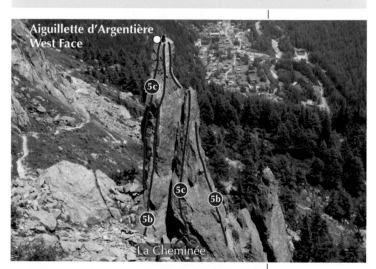

Aiguillette d'Argentière
West Face

La Cheminée

There are more routes on this needle of rock that you might imagine. Let's just concentrate on the path-side (W) face (going towards the ladders), which has four good routes from grade 4 to 5 (topo). The most spectacular one

*Making the awkward but quite spectacular step
on the Aiguillette d'Argentière*

is La Cheminée, which as its name suggests starts up a chimney but then leaves it to continue up the slab on the right, topping out onto a pillar. A somewhat bold move here allows the main needle to be regained and this is climbed to the top.

# AREA 6
*Vallorcine Slab (Rocher de la Saix)*

| | |
|---|---|
| **Start** | Vallorcine train station |
| **Guidebook** | *Crag Climbing in Chamonix* by François Burnier and Dominique Potard |
| **Access** | Walk over the level crossing and take the track on the right, which leads through a meadow. A little further on the path up to the crag is signed on the left (10min). |
| **Rope required** | Double 50m ropes |

This is a great cliff for easier climbs, even though there are also some harder more technical routes. This is moderate climbing as it should be – lots of holds, good lines and just steep enough to feel that little bit physical. Multi-pitch.

Be warned, this crag can get very busy due to the quality of its rock and ease of access, but recently it seems to be that little bit quieter.

There are lots of routes here, probably too many as it all gets very confusing and once again the Chamonix guidebook is inaccurate. I've described just two really good routes up the right-hand pillar, but you'll find lots of other reasonably graded climbs in the guidebook. There are also some harder technical slab pitches which are good quality.

The right-hand pillar described is the first part of the cliff to dry after rain, which is worth bearing in mind.

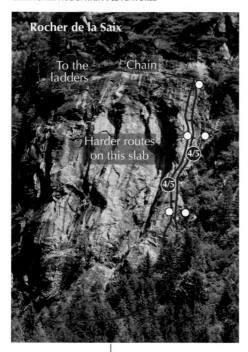

Rocher de la Saix

To the ladders

Chain

Harder routes on this slab

4/5

4/5

It's best to gear up at the main area before walking up to the start of these two climbs as the descent brings you back to the main area. At the base of the cliff look for a small path which heads off to the right into the vegetation – watch out for nettles. This leads unpleasantly but quickly to a clearing where two lines of bolts head up the face. The left one has another route, which breaks out of it after the second bolt.

Basically the two right-most routes give great three-pitch climbs of a fairly consistent grade 4/5. It's quite confusing as there are several lines but just stick to the pillar. In the middle the two routes briefly join up before going their separate ways higher up. There are two belay stations on each route, each less than 50m apart.

Unless there is no-one else climbing on the pillar, the safest way to descend is to follow the descent route – carry up your trainers. This route is equipped. Follow the chains at the top of the cliff left towards a series of ladders then a path which brings you back to the foot of the crag.

Abseil descent is feasible with two 50m ropes if there is no-one below. From the belay at the top of the pillar descend to the two bolt belays then do a second abseil heading slightly right (looking out) to a large ledge where there are at least three metal stanchion anchors. From here one more abseil leads to the ground.

*Starting the chains descent at Vallorcine*

 **AREA 7**

*Barberine*

| | |
|---|---|
| **Start** | Bridge just outside Barberine village |
| **Guidebook** | Barberine is just the first part of a extensive group of cliffs which are documented in the English/French guidebook *Les classiques et les nouveaux spots de Barberine Giétroz* by Jon de Montjoye. |
| **Access** | Drive through Vallorcine and turn left just before the Franco-Swiss frontier, signed to Barberine. Park on the right before the bridge that leads to the village. Walk through the village and take a trail that goes right next to a house with a plaque on it. Go down the field and over the river then out into a clearing. Go back into the forest just near two benches, following a trail up left towards the base of the cliff. |
| **Rope required** | A single 60m rope. The two routes described here climb good clean rock. Further left there is an old vegetated and abandoned route, so don't be confused by any fixed gear you might see there. |

Some nice friction slabs for those who like that sort of thing. Some routes also have holds! Multi-pitch.

Two of the best and most reasonable routes on these lower slabs are over on the left.

From the base of the slabs scramble up to the left over tree roots to a blocky ledge. There is a line of bolts directly above – this is the left-most route and is 5+. Climb up and pass just left of the obvious overlap.

The line of bolts to the right gives another good route of grade 6a, starting down to the right, from the ground, and heads directly up and over an overlap, which gives the crux.

*Looking down to the lower Barberine slabs from one of the longer Barberine routes (photo: Marc Volorio)*

Both routes join at the belay above the overlap. A short pitch leads to a cable hand-line. Once there it's advisable to walk off easily along ledges to the right, rather than abseiling back down, so as not to disturb other climbers. This can be done easily in rock boots – if

*Perfect rock on the Barberine cliffs*

you can bear the pain. If you feel you must abseil back down the routes then you will need two 50m ropes to do so.

There are lots of other good slab routes and excellent multi-pitch routes if you climb grade 6 – see the guide-book for details.

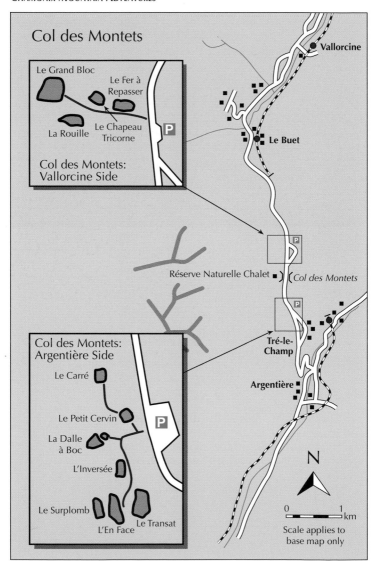

Col des Montets

Le Grand Bloc
Le Fer à Repasser
La Rouille
Le Chapeau Tricorne

Col des Montets: Vallorcine Side

Col des Montets: Argentière Side

Le Carré
Le Petit Cervin
La Dalle à Boc
L'Inversée
Le Surplomb
L'En Face
Le Transat

Vallorcine

Le Buet

Réserve Naturelle Chalet

Col des Montets

Tré-le-Champ

Argentière

N

0    1 km

Scale applies to base map only

# BOULDERING

##  AREA 1
*Col des Montets*

| | |
|---|---|
| **Start** | Argentière side: car park on the right (coming from Chamonix) 300m before the col; Vallorcine side: parking spaces 200m beyond the col on the right. |

The col has boulders strewn all over it but for the purposes of bouldering it's divided into two sides, the Argentière side and the Vallorcine side – see topo. The problems are too numerous to list here so I've chosen just a few classics on both sides. These are of a moderate grade but there are problems to suit all abilities, from beginners and children to hardened crag rats, and the site continues to evolve as new generations of young climbers hone their skills there.

### Argentière side
This side of the pass has lots of different boulders, all of which have some moderate problems among the harder ones. Cross the road and take a path through the bushes, which leads to the boulders. This is the road pass between the Chamonix valley and the Vallorcine valley.

### Le Petit Cervin
This boulder is very obvious from the road. It has three routes up the front face that are 4c to 5c. A top rope can be rigged up by passing a rope over the top and belaying from the other side.

### Le Transat
The most popular boulder on the col, the north face has lots of reasonable routes while the south face is harder. There are a couple of metal anchors for top-roping.

### L'en face

A nice boulder with some good problems in the 5–6 range, the Grosse Ecaille being a classic.

### Vallorcine side

This side has some bigger boulders, notably the Grand Bloc, where it's common to see top ropes set up on the easy problems of the west face. Most of the other problems are harder on excellent rough gneiss. Cross the road to reach the boulders, the Grand Bloc being easy to spot.

### Grand Bloc

The west face is very good for beginner climbers and a top rope can easily be installed. The south-west face has some excellent harder routes, which are generally done on top rope.

*Bouldering is the simplest of activities and one of the most intense (photo: Marc Volorio)*

 **AREA 2**

*Pierre d'Orthaz*

| | |
|---|---|
| **Start** | Hotel de l'Arveyron car park |
| **Access** | From Chamonix take the road towards Argentière. After 1.5km take the small road on the right signed 'Orthaz', where it ends at the Hotel de l'Arveyron. Continue 150m on foot to a clearing where this iconic boulder will be found. |

This boulder is situated in the Bois de Bouchet forest just outside Chamonix and in the 1960s and 1970s enjoyed an iconic status in Chamonix. It boasts several hard and strenuous problems with some high finishes.

## 🏵 AREA 3
*Les Bossons*

*Good spotting on the En Face at the Col des Montets*

| | |
|---|---|
| **Start** | Parking area beneath the Glacier des Bossons |
| **Access** | Take the Les Bossons turn off on the N205. Follow the Route des Rives leading up the hill, past the Gîte la Crémerie du Glacier. At the road junction take the Chemin du Cerro and follow this upwards (past four junctions) until it finishes at a small parking area 20m before a large pylon. The first boulder is a 1min walk through the trees, on the left of the main path. |

**AREA 4**

*Le Coupeau*

| | |
|---|---|
| **Start** | Le Coupeau, near the archery zone |
| **Access** | Take the road on the opposite side of the valley from Les Houches towards Merlet and Le Coupeau. After the first two bends park near to the archery zone. Take the path which goes into the forest and after 5min, at a clearing, you'll see the number 20 painted on a tree and a rock. This is the first sector; 5min further takes you to the other sector, the Bloc Pascal. |

Lots of boulders strewn around the forest give a great variety of problems at all grades in a pleasant environment.

 **AREA 5**

*Le Médonnet*

| | |
|---|---|
| **Start** | Car park 200m before the Chapelle de Médonnet |
| **Access** | From Sallanches, follow the N212 towards Megève. After 3km turn right towards Cordon Natcruy. About 300m further on there is a small car park, 200m before the Chapelle de Médonnet. |

This is regarded as one of the best bouldering sites in the region, with rock reminiscent of Fontainebleau. The boulders are nicely shaded by trees, making it a good site for the summer.

# 6 VIA FERRATAS

High up on one of the brilliant traverses at Le Mont

Via ferratas today are fun, equipped routes for people seeking the thrill of climbing up rock faces without the technical skills required in rock climbing. The historical background of via ferratas is rather different. In 1914 via ferrata routes were created in the Dolomites by the Italian army, to help move troops and equipment (including artillery) from one side of a mountain to the other.

When the war was over the Dolomites' via ferratas were abandoned by the army, but local people maintained them. The Italian Alpine Club soon recognised the value of these routes and began to create new ones to attract tourists. The term 'via ferrata' is an archaism (it literally translates as 'iron-equipped route' or 'improved way'), and was the original name for the military routes, but in popular parlance this is the name used to describe these adventurous routes which are now climbed for pleasure.

In France, the first via ferrata was built in 1989 in the Alps, solely for the purpose of having fun and providing a new way of discovering the mountains. In the Chamonix valley there aren't actually any via ferrata routes, perhaps because all the cliffs are used by rock climbers. However, you don't have to drive too far from

Chamonix to find some good ones. Two are described here and several others are noted. Up-to-date information for the via ferratas described here, plus many others throughout France, can be found on this website www. viaferrata-fr.net.

Despite not requiring the technical skills of rock climbing, via ferratas tend to go into very impressive areas of rock and can be extremely intimidating. One mistake could be fatal so it's essential to know how to use the gear. The equipment required is:

- harness
- helmet
- via ferrata lanyard

*A dedicated via ferrata lanyard is essential kit*

The lanyard comes equipped with two karabiners, one of which should always be attached to a line or bolt. The lanyard itself consists of two slings with an energy absorber – a length of tape or rope or other friction brake system. If a fall occurs, the spare tape or rope will unravel or the friction device will come into play, bringing dynamic force into the system. Do

not be tempted to use a regular rock-climbing sling and karabiner – this is not adequate as a fall on a via ferrata will exert huge force onto the sling, and hence onto the person falling, and could result in a broken back.

Many people rope together to do via ferratas, which is advisable if you have different levels of experience and confidence in the group. But roping together increases risk in the case of a fall so it is crucial to be familiar with this technique.

Some of the via ferratas require some strenuous steps and long reaches so you need to look carefully at the description for the route you're going for. Most via ferratas are graded from F (*facile*) up to ED (*extrêmement difficile*).

*Those rungs just beckon you along …*

It's quite scary to look down ...

Bear in mind that an hour or so of pulling yourself up ladders and rungs can be pretty tiring and will probably be enough for most people. Moreover in high summer a south-facing cliff will be very hot and so you'll need to take water and probably a snack.

Bike gloves are useful as the cables are hard on the hands, but don't be tempted to take wool or fleece gloves or ski mitts!

If you're a beginner to via ferratas you are strongly recommended to hire a qualified guide who will show you exactly how to use the gear and also how to climb in an efficient way without getting too exhausted.

The technical descriptions for the via ferratas here have been taken from the official information provided by the local tourist offices. They all advise against taking children, but photos of the routes often show kids and the local guides definitely do lead youngsters on these via ferratas. Whether children should be taken depends on several factors:

- The age and size of the child. There is a minimum size as the child has to be able to reach the holds!
- Does the child want to do it – many tears are shed on via ferratas (not just by children!). Escape is often not an option once embarked on those scary traverses and climbs.
- Can the child be relied on to not make a mistake clipping and unclipping. An error will usually have drastic consequences.

#  ROUTE 1

## *Le Mont, Sixt-Fer-à-Cheval*

| | |
|---|---|
| **Start** | Parking des Tines, 3km from Samoëns |
| **Grade** | AD/D/AD |
| **Time** | Approach: 20min; route: 1hr 20min; return: 20min |
| **Altitude range** | 860m–1010m |
| **Access** | From Samoëns take the road towards Sixt-Fer-à-Cheval and look out for the Parking des Tines on the right after 3km or so. To reach the base of the via ferrata cross the road and follow a path into the woods which leads to the route in about 20min. This path is slippery after rain. |
| **Note** | Open from March to November. Not suitable for children. |

This fine via ferrata overlooks the Gorges des Tines, near to the spectacular cirque of Sixt-Fer-à-Cheval. The route doesn't present too many difficulties but is quite exposed and airy. However, it is split into sections so escape is possible along the way.

The route can be divided into three parts – hence the three grades – with the avoidable middle section being the hardest.

The first part begins with a long easy ledge (the 'bears' ledge'), which leads to the base of a cave. Next follows a 10m vertical wall, followed by another traverse with an overhang this time. Here there is a choice. You can finish and join the path, or take a shortcut to re-join the route for the final part. Or continue towards the right on the main route.

The second part begins with a pleasant, gently ascending traverse, which is very airy. This takes you to a bridge. Next there's another ledge, then an 8m ladder and finally a traverse across a slab to a fun, steep wall, which exits onto the descent path.

A 50m walk down this path leads to the final part of the route (at the escape point at the top of the first part). Midway along the walk be careful not to mistake an

*It can get quite busy on via ferratas in the holidays, here at Le Mont Sixt*

escape route cable for this continuation – keep going on the path until the 'Vire du Raffour' is signed. This last part, which is quite long, consists of a long traverse (the 'Vire du Raffour'), which is very exposed and has some overhanging sections. A short ascent is encountered before the end.

To descend, follow the descent path towards the left with some very easy cabled sections – it joins the ascent path further down.

##  ROUTE 2
*La Curalla, Passy*

| | |
|---|---|
| **Start** | Car park 200m above Plateau d'Assy |
| **Grade** | AD |
| **Time** | Approach: 20min; route: 1hr; return: 40min |
| **Altitude range** | 1300m–1420m |

| | |
|---|---|
| **Access** | From Passy drive up to the Plateau d'Assy and look out for a left turn signed to the via ferrata. The car park is 200m higher. The gear rental is beyond the car park on the main track. There is an information board about the via ferrata in the car park. To reach the start take the forest track which leaves the car park and after 150m go right following fluorescent yellow marks up to the start of the via ferrata at the foot of the cliff (20min, of which 15min are steep). |
| **Note** | Open from May to September. Not suitable for children. |

This via ferrata is situated at the Plateau d'Assy, above Passy on the lower ramparts of the Aiguille de Varan. It's on a south-facing cliff with Mont Blanc opposite, so the situation is quite stunning. The equipment is well placed and in good condition, which all makes for a classic via ferrata experience. It takes an hour to climb and given the sunny situation this is long enough. There are few rests on the route and no escape routes.

Near the car park there is a small cabin where you can rent via ferrata lanyards. This is not in the car park itself, but just up the hill on the right. Drinks can also be bought here.

*The wobbly Nepalese bridge at Curalla provides some fun (photo: Roger Portch)*

*Enjoying the Curalla Via Ferrata at Passy*

The fun starts as soon as you leave the ground, with a steep section of rungs leading up the cliff. Quite soon you'll reach a Nepalese bridge – four people is the maximum load at a time. The far end is high and you need a good long lanyard. Rungs continue, then a plank as a monkey bridge followed by two more planks a lot further on. Near the end the route goes around an exposed arête onto a different face to finish.

For the descent, follow the well-marked path towards the right at the top. It becomes a steep forest track and leads back to the car park.

# OTHER ROUTES IN THE HAUTE SAVOIE REGION

*A calm and relaxed approach generally works best*

The following via ferratas are within driving distance of Chamonix. The brief descriptions are taken from the local topos and have not been verified.

**ROUTE 3**

*La Yves Pollet Villard, La Clusaz*

| | |
|---|---|
| **Start** | Car park below Col des Aravis |
| **Grade** | D/F/D+ |
| **Time** | Approach: 20min; route: 3hr; return: 45min |
| **Altitude range** | 1530m–1830m |
| **Access** | From La Clusaz take the road for the Col des Aravis. The car park has a via ferrata sign and is on the left on the first bends towards the col. From the car park follow a path which goes up towards the climbing cliff, then heads off right to reach the start of the via ferrata. |
| **Note** | Open from May to November. Not suitable for children. |

This long via ferrata has no escape route other than the choice of finish.

A long ascending traverse rather than a vertical ascent, rather similar to some of the Dolomites routes, using natural ledges and vertical walls, with a great bridge. The route is quite exposed in its second half. There are two possible exits: on the right an easy finish, on the left an overhang giving the D+ grade, but well equipped.

Descent is by a good path on the left leads that via the Combe de Borderan to the car park.

# 🅖 ROUTE 4
*La Roche à l'Agathe, Thônes*

| | |
|---|---|
| **Start** | Car park near Thones bus station |
| **Grade** | PD/D/D+ or ED |
| **Time** | Approach: 10min; route: 1hr 30min; return: 30min |
| **Altitude range** | 665m–895m |
| **Access** | The most user-friendly car park is found by going left at the first roundabout encountered when coming to Thônes from Annecy. There are signs for the via ferrata parking near to the bus station. Leave the car here then continue on foot through the subway to the end of the road. From there a sign indicates the path on the right, which zigzags up for 10min in the forest. |
| **Note** | Open from May to October. Not suitable for children. |

A fairly airy route. Being at low altitude it can get very hot.

The first part of the route is quite exposed but not too athletic. A monkey bridge and several vertical to overhanging walls must be overcome, but there is an escape route before things get any harder.

The second part is very athletic and is not for beginners – overhanging walls and lots of exposure lead to a ledge where there are three choices for the continuation. One is to take the escape route on the right; a second option is to climb the ladder which overlooks the void and Thônes itself; or the third choice – for those with very strong arms – is to tackle the overhang (Surplomb de l'Ermite) which is graded ED.

To descend follow the cabled descent route, which joins the route to the Chapelle du Calvaire then goes back to the car park.

# APPENDIX A
*Useful contacts*

Please note that telephone numbers may change. The numbers below were correct at the time of writing (October 2011). All numbers are noted for calling from France. If calling a French number from outside France, dial the international dialling code (00 in Europe), add 33 (the national code for France) and then dial the number, omitting the first zero.

**Tourist offices**

Chamonix Tourist Office
www.chamonix.com
Tel 04 50 53 00 24

Argentière Tourist Office
www.chamonix.com
Tel 04 50 54 02 14

Vallorcine Tourist Office
www.vallorcine.com
Tel 04 50 54 60 71

Les Houches Tourist Office
www.leshouches.com
Tel 04 50 545 50 62

Servoz Tourist Office
www.leshouches.com
Tel 04 50 47 21 68

Passy Tourist Office
www.passy-mont-blanc.com
Tel 04 50 58 80 52

Saint-Gervais-les-Bains Tourist Office
www.saintgervais.com
Tel 04 50 47 76 08

**Mountain information and guides**

Office de Haute Montagne
www.ohm-chamonix.com
Tel 04 50 53 22 08

Compagnie des Guides Chamonix
www.chamonix-guides.com
Tel 04 50 53 00 88

Compagnie des Guides Saint Gervais les Bains
www.guides-mont-blanc.com
Tel 04 50 47 76 55

Trekking in the Alps
www.trekkinginthealps.com
Tel 06 82 65 42 14

**Alpine huts**

Refuge Albert Premier
Tel 04 50 54 06 20

Refuge d'Argentière
Tel 04 50 53 16 92

Chalet de la Balme
Tel 04 50 47 03 54

Refuge Bel Lachat
Tel 04 50 53 43 23

## *Chamonix Mountain Adventures*

Auberge de Bionnassay
Tel 04 50 93 45 23

Auberge La Boerne Tré-le-Champ
Tel 04 50 54 05 14

Refuge de la Charpoua
Tel 046 87 99 01 66

Refuge Col de Balme
Tel 04 50 54 02 33

Hotel Col de la Forclaz
Tel 0041 27 722 2688

Refuge des Cosmiques
Tel 04 50 54 40 16

Refuge du Couvercle
Tel 04 50 53 16 94

Refuge de Doran
Tel 04 50 58 08 00

Refuge de la Flégère
Tel 06 03 58 28 14

Refuge du Goûter
Tel 04 50 54 40 93

Chalet du Lac Blanc
Tel 04 50 53 49 14

Refuge de Lognan
Tel 06 88 56 03 54

Refuge de Loriaz
Tel 04 50 54 06 45

Chalet de Miage
Tel 04 50 93 22 91

Refuge Moëde d'Anterne
Tel 04 50 93 60 43

Refuge Nant Borrant
Tel 04 50 47 03 57

Cabane d'Orny
Tel 0041 27 783 1887

Refuge de la Pierre à Bérard
Tel 04 50 54 62 08

Refuge du Plan de l'Aiguille
Tel 06 65 64 27 53

Refuge de Platé
Tel 04 50 93 11 07

Hotel Prarion
Tel 04 50 54 40 07

Refuge de Tête Rousse
Tel 04 50 58 24 97

Rifugio Torino
Tel 0039 340 22 70 121

Refuge de Tré-la-Tête
Tel 04 50 47 01 68

Cabane du Trient
Tel 0041 27 783 1438

Chalet du Truc
Tel 04 50 93 12 48

Cabane du Vieux Emosson
Tel 0041 27 768 1421

**Bike shops**
**Chamonix**
Intersport
240 route du Bouchet
Tel 04 50 47 73 50

Legend'chx
Avenue de l'Aiguille du Midi
Tel 04 50 90 22 25
www.legendchx.com

Le Grand Bi
240 avenue du Bouchet
Tel 04 50 53 14 16

Ski Max
Passage Androsace
Tel 04 50 96 15 92

Zero G
90 avenue Ravanel le Rouge
Tel 04 50 53 01 01
www.zerogchx.com

**Argentière**
Pezier Sports
620 route de Plagnolet
Tel 04 50 54 68 48
www.pezier-sports.com

**Vallorcine**
Sanglard Sports Residence Mont Blanc
Tel 04 50 21 34 65
www.vallorcine.skimium.fr/

Serge Filipelli at the Vallorcine cable car
Tel 04 50 89 21 61

**Les Houches**
Cyprien Sports – Skimium
244 rue de l'Essert
Tel 04 50 54 41 02
www.cypriensports.com

MG Sport
11 rue de l'Essert
Tel 04 57 19 94 89
www.m-g-sport.com

**Mountain bike lift pass**
This pass requires a photo and is non-transferable. It cost €18 for one day in 2011. The pass gives unlimited access to the following lifts:

- Chamonix – Planpraz cable car
- Les Praz – La Flégère cable car
- Argentière – Lognan cable car
- Le Tour – Charamillon cable car
- Balme chairlift (at Le Tour)
- Vallorcine – Posettes cable car
- Les Houches – Prarion cable car.

# APPENDIX B
*Useful French words and phrases*

## Weather

| | |
|---|---|
| weather | *le temps* |
| forecast | *la prévision* |
| hot | *chaud* |
| cold | *froid* |
| sunny | *ensoleillé* |
| rainy | *pluvieux* |
| windy | *venté* |
| cloudy | *nuageux* |
| fog | *le brouillard* |
| stormy | *orageux* |
| snowy | *enneigé* |
| temperature | *la température* |
| changeable | *variable* |
| thunder | *la tonnerre* |
| lightning | *l'éclair* |
| gusts/gales | *les rafales* |
| white out | *jour blanc* |
| ice | *la glace* |
| verglace | *le verglas* |
| hail | *la grêle* |
| freezing | *glacial* |
| starry | *étoillé* |

## Emergencies

| | |
|---|---|
| Help! | *au secours!* |
| accident | *un accident* |
| emergency | *une urgence* |
| stop | *halte* |
| quick | *vite* |
| be careful | *faites attention* |
| rescue | *secours* |
| helicopter | *l'helicoptère* |
| ambulance | *l'ambulance* |
| hospital | *hôpital* |
| doctor | *le médecin* |

| | |
|---|---|
| heart attack | *la crise cardiaque* |
| broken arm/leg | *le bras/la jambe cassé(e)* |
| asthma attack | *la crise d'asthme* |
| I am lost | *je suis perdu* |

## Climbing/via ferrata equipment

| | |
|---|---|
| harness | *baudrier* |
| lanyard | *la longe* |
| helmet | *le casque* |
| karabiner | *le mousqueton* |

## Lifts

| | |
|---|---|
| cable car | *le téléphérique* |
| gondola | *la télécabine* |
| chairlift | *le télésiège* |
| drag-lift | *le téléski* |

## Other useful words

| | |
|---|---|
| open | *ouvert* |
| closed | *fermé* |

The following terms may need some explanation. They are used throughout the book.

*Alpage* – A summer farm usually above the treeline. The cattle are brought up here for the months of July and August to graze.

*Col* – A pass or a saddle

*Cwm/corrie/combe* – A basin formed around three sides by hills or mountains. It can be steep sided or more gently rounded.

*Névé* – Snow that fell in the winter but has remained well into the summer months.

# APPENDIX C
*Further reading*

*Mont Blanc Walks* Hilary Sharp (Cicerone Press, 2010)

*Mountain Bike Guide Chamonix Mont Blanc* Tom Wilson-North (Mountain Drop Offs UK, 2008)

*Crag Climbing in Chamonix* François Burnier and Dominique Potar (Vamos, 2005)

*The Aiguilles Rouges 1* Michel Piola (Editions Michel Piola, 2007)

*Les classiques et les nouveaux spots de Barberine Giétroz* Jon de Montjoye (Montjoye, 2006)

*Cycling in the French Alps* Paul Henderson (Cicerone Press, 2008)

# APPENDIX D
*Glacier travel and rescue techniques*

While there are plenty of non-glaciated summits to tackle on snowshoes, you may eventually choose to go higher and experience the high mountain environment. This is the realm of glaciers, which introduce a whole new dimension into snowshoeing, notably that of the dangers of crevasses. With the right equipment and, far more importantly, with the right knowledge, these dangers can be reduced to an acceptable level. This knowledge can be gained in part from books, but there is really no substitute for experience – either going with experienced friends or by paying for professional instruction by qualified guides. **It is essential that you are experienced in glacier travel before venturing onto any of the glaciated walks in this book.**

The principal hazard of glacier travel is that of hidden crevasses. On a dry glacier (i.e. a glacier not covered with snow) crevasses are obvious and therefore pose no problems. However, on a wet (snow-covered) glacier what lurks beneath the surface presents a very real danger.

Travel on a wet glacier is always undertaken roped together – even if there is a good track and good visibility. Roping up wrongly and/or using the rope incorrectly can make any crevasse incident worse. It is therefore essential to adopt correct practice and to keep to certain guidelines.

**This following information is not intended as an instruction manual for the novice, but as a reminder for those who already have these skills.**

Glacier travel and crevasse rescue techniques must be learnt and practised, either on a specialised course or from an experienced mountaineer or a professional.

Glacier travel and rescue procedures for a party of two people are described below. Each participant should be equipped with the minimum of an ice-axe, a harness and screwgate krab, an ice screw, a 120cm sling, three prussik loops, a pulley and three spare karabiners. The party should have a dynamic rope, the minimum diameter of which should be 8mm, though in practice a larger diameter is more user-friendly when it comes to handling in a crevasse-rescue situation. It is not necessary to have a designated single rope of 10mm or 11mm if only pure glacier travel is envisaged. The minimum length should be about 30m for two people. For larger numbers a longer rope or two ropes should be used.

The walkers should be roped together with about 10m of rope between them. To do this each should tie into the ends of the rope and take an equal number of coils around their

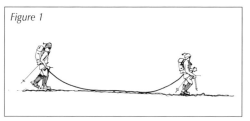

Figure 1

shoulders until the middle 10m is left. The coils are tied off by passing a bight of rope around them and tying an overhand knot around the rope that leads between the walkers. This leaves a loop which can be clipped back into the harness with the screwgate karabiner.

## WALKING ON THE GLACIER

When walking the rope should be kept reasonably tight – so that only the middle 5–6m glide along the snow (see Figure 1). If this tension is maintained, not only will the rope be kept away from sharp crampons but it also avoids the dangerous practice of walkers holding the rope up in their hand, which can result in a serious shoulder injury in the event of a crevasse fall.

One trekking pole should be stowed away on the rucksack leaving that hand free for the ice-axe. The axe **must** be instantly available for arresting a fall, not attached to the back of the rucksack. It should be carried by the head, with the shaft downwards like a walking stick, in the uphill hand whenever appropriate.

Two further refinements of this basic system are the pre-attachment of prussik loops to the rope and the tying of knots in the rope at intervals along the 10m. The theory behind the latter method is that in the event of a crevasse fall the rope will cut into the snow lip and the knot will jam into the snow, thus arresting the fall. The downside of this system is that if the snow is very soft the knot will pass right through the snow and will hinder the consequent rescue.

It is worth considering putting the lightest person at the front, as disparity in weight is an important factor – if the lighter person falls in the crevasse the heavier person will find it easier to pull him out. But bear in mind that it is not always the first person to cross that breaks a fragile snowbridge.

Although both members of the party should be vigilant at all times on a glacier, some particularly crevassed areas will obviously be more dangerous than others. This information should be passed back from the leader so that the second person can prepare himself and tighten the rope further.

## ARRESTING A FALL

The first reaction to one of the walkers falling into a crevasse can determine success or failure. If the other person is pulled flat on his face, then arresting the fall becomes very difficult. The ideal reaction is to jerk backwards and adopt a semi-sitting

*Figure 2*

The basic belay for crevasse rescue in snow is the horizontally buried ice-axe (see Figure 3). If the snow isn't deep enough then this is where the ice screw comes in. A slot must first be cut, using the axe, at right angles to the pull of the rope and as deep as possible. It should be the length of the axe and the forward wall should be slightly incut to avoid the axe being pulled out. A second slot, this time in line with the pull, should be cut, thus forming a T. It must be the same depth as the first slot and should rise to the surface at as shallow an angle as possible. Doing this is not easy, and is furthered hindered by the coils around the rescuer's shoulders. These

position, with the shaft of the axe plunged into the snow (see Figure 2). At this point it will be best to remove snowshoes to enable heels to kick in to provide a solid stance.

Before doing anything else the rescuer should do the following.

1  Shout to try to make contact with the victim – it may well be that by lowering him slightly he will be able to walk out of the crevasse on the other side.

2  Look around for other people – a group of 4–5 will be able to use brute force to pull the victim up or, at worst, help in the following stages of the rescue.

3  Ascertain whether it is possible for the victim to ascend the rope using his prussik loops, assuming he knows how to do this.

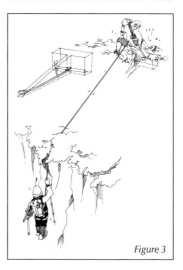

*Figure 3*

can be slipped over the head to leave the upper body free.

When the slot is prepared, a Larks Foot or Clove Hitch is put around the axe at approximately two-thirds of the way up the shaft towards the head (this is to provide an equal bearing surface to prevent the axe from pivoting). The axe is pushed horizontally into the head of the slot and the sling laid into the right-angle slot. A krab is clipped to the sling. A prussik loop is tied in an autobloc/French prussik around the tight rope as close as possible to the krab and then clipped to this. Now the prussik is pushed forward as tight as possible, and the rescuer should slide forward gently to transfer the victim's weight to the autobloc. The shoulder coils can be undone and removed methodically, and finally the rope on the slack side of the autobloc should be clipped through the krab. This is now referred to as a clutch.

Figure 4

## PREPARATION FOR HOISTING

For the rescuer to operate in safety he must be attached to the belay (see Figure 4). The easiest way to do this is to untie from the end of the rope and clip this to the belay. He should then attach himself to the rope via an Italian Hitch into the screwgate krab on his harness. He must carefully approach the edge of the crevasse, paying out the rope through the hitch (effectively abseiling though not necessarily weighting the belay). Having ascertained that the victim needs

pulling out, the edge of the crevasse must be prepared by pushing trekking poles under the rope as near to the edge as possible to prevent further cutting into the lip. The remaining snow lip can be broken away. The frightened victim must now be told to remove his snowshoes and to clip these, along with his ice-axe and pole, to his harness.

## THE 3:1 HOIST

If the rope hasn't bitten too far into the lip, or if the weight/strength difference of the walkers isn't to the rescuer's disadvantage, it should be possible to lift the victim using a 3:1 pulley system (sometimes referred to as a Z pulley) (see Figure 5a). A second prussik loop is tied onto the

See Figure 5c

See Figure 5b

Figure 5a

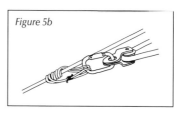

Figure 5b

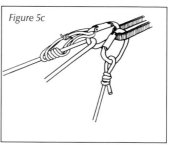

Figure 5c

taut rope close to the poles at the lip, and a krab and pulley clipped to it. The slack rope from the clutch can now be clipped through the pulley. Pulling the rope back towards the belay now gives a mechanical advantage of 3:1. As the victim moves upwards the autobloc forming the clutch slackens and allows the rope to run through it. When the rescuer tires he can gently release the load and the clutch will reactivate and hold the victim's weight again. Similarly, when the pulley has been pulled up tight against the belay, the clutch can be used to hold the victim whilst the pulley is slid back down the rope to start again.

### THE 6:1 HOIST

If the 3:1 hoist doesn't work it can be quickly turned into a 6:1 (see Figure 6). The third prussik loop is tied onto the rope as it exits the pulley, and the third krab is clipped to it. The other end of the rope, which up to now has protected the rescuer, can be clipped through the third krab. Pulling on this results in a 6:1 system. The rescuer will have a fair amount of running around to do, as for every 6m of rope he pulls in the victim will rise only 1m.

Finally, as the victim nears the lip the rescuer will have to try to extract the rope from where it has bitten in by pulling and bracing his feet against the wall of the crevasse. At the last moment the rescuer may be able to crawl forward to help the victim out.

## GLACIER TRAVEL CHECKLIST

- Crampons
- Ice-axe – 55–60cm for a normal-sized person
- Harness

Crevasse rescue equipment:
- 2 prussik loops
- long sling
- 5 karabiners (1 screw-gate, 1 pear-shaped screwgate (HMS) which can be used for an Italian hitch, 3 snaplinks)
- ice screw.

This is a minimum of rescue equipment, and you may choose to take other things.
- Rope – this should be a dynamic rope of at least 8mm, and a minimum of about 30m long. Clearly if there are lots of people in the group more than one rope should be taken, but bear in mind that weight is also an issue. Note that the downside of a thin rope is that it is harder to grip for rescue manoeuvres, both by hand and with prussiks.

Finally, be sure to practise all glacier travel techniques before venturing onto glacier terrain.

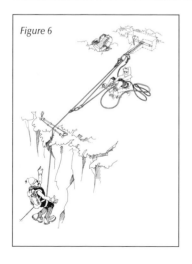

Figure 6

# NOTES

# NOTES

# NOTES

# LISTING OF CICERONE GUIDES

## BRITISH ISLES CHALLENGES, COLLECTIONS AND ACTIVITIES

Cycling Land's End to John o' Groats
Great Walks on the England Coast Path
The Big Rounds
The Book of the Bivvy
The Book of the Bothy
The Mountains of England & Wales:
  Vol 1 Wales
  Vol 2 England
The National Trails
Walking The End to End Trail

## SCOTLAND

Ben Nevis and Glen Coe
Cycle Touring in Northern Scotland
Cycling in the Hebrides
Great Mountain Days in Scotland
Mountain Biking in Southern and Central Scotland
Mountain Biking in West and North West Scotland
Not the West Highland Way
Scotland
Scotland's Mountain Ridges
Scottish Wild Country Backpacking
Skye's Cuillin Ridge Traverse
The Borders Abbeys Way
The Great Glen Way
The Great Glen Way Map Booklet
The Hebridean Way
The Hebrides
The Isle of Mull
The Isle of Skye
The Skye Trail
The Southern Upland Way
The Speyside Way
The Speyside Way Map Booklet
The West Highland Way
The West Highland Way Map Booklet
Walking Ben Lawers, Rannoch and Atholl
Walking in the Cairngorms
Walking in the Pentland Hills
Walking in the Scottish Borders
Walking in the Southern Uplands
Walking in Torridon, Fisherfield, Fannichs and An Teallach
Walking Loch Lomond and the Trossachs
Walking on Arran
Walking on Harris and Lewis
Walking on Jura, Islay and Colonsay
Walking on Rum and the Small Isles
Walking on the Orkney and Shetland Isles
Walking on Uist and Barra
Walking the Cape Wrath Trail

Walking the Corbetts
  Vol 1 South of the Great Glen
  Vol 2 North of the Great Glen
Walking the Galloway Hills
Walking the Munros
  Vol 1 – Southern, Central and Western Highlands
  Vol 2 – Northern Highlands and the Cairngorms
Winter Climbs Ben Nevis and Glen Coe

## NORTHERN ENGLAND ROUTES

Cycling the Reivers Route
Cycling the Way of the Roses
Hadrian's Cycleway
Hadrian's Wall Path
Hadrian's Wall Path Map Booklet
The C2C Cycle Route
The Coast to Coast Map Booklet
The Coast to Coast Walk
The Pennine Way
The Pennine Way Map Booklet
Walking the Dales Way
Walking the Dales Way Map Booklet

## NORTH-EAST ENGLAND, YORKSHIRE DALES AND PENNINES

Cycling in the Yorkshire Dales
Great Mountain Days in the Pennines
Mountain Biking in the Yorkshire Dales
St Oswald's Way and St Cuthbert's Way
The Cleveland Way and the Yorkshire Wolds Way
The Cleveland Way Map Booklet
The North York Moors
The Reivers Way
Trail and Fell Running in the Yorkshire Dales
Walking in County Durham
Walking in Northumberland
Walking in the North Pennines
Walking in the Yorkshire Dales: North and East
Walking in the Yorkshire Dales: South and West

## NORTH-WEST ENGLAND AND THE ISLE OF MAN

Cycling the Pennine Bridleway
Isle of Man Coastal Path
The Lancashire Cycleway
The Lune Valley and Howgills
Walking in Cumbria's Eden Valley
Walking in Lancashire

Walking in the Forest of Bowland and Pendle
Walking on the Isle of Man
Walking on the West Pennine Moors
Walks in Silverdale and Arnside

## LAKE DISTRICT

Cycling in the Lake District
Great Mountain Days in the Lake District
Joss Naylor's Lakes, Meres and Waters of the Lake District
Lake District Winter Climbs
Lake District: High Level and Fell Walks
Lake District: Low Level and Lake Walks
Mountain Biking in the Lake District
Outdoor Adventures with Children – Lake District
Scrambles in the Lake District – North
Scrambles in the Lake District – South
Trail and Fell Running in the Lake District
Walking The Cumbria Way
Walking the Lake District Fells –
  Borrowdale
  Buttermere
  Coniston
  Keswick
  Langdale
  Mardale and the Far East
  Patterdale
  Wasdale
Walking the Tour of the Lake District

## DERBYSHIRE, PEAK DISTRICT AND MIDLANDS

Cycling in the Peak District
Dark Peak Walks
Scrambles in the Dark Peak
Walking in Derbyshire
Walking in the Peak District – White Peak East
Walking in the Peak District – White Peak West

## SOUTHERN ENGLAND

20 Classic Sportive Rides in South East England
20 Classic Sportive Rides in South West England
Cycling in the Cotswolds
Mountain Biking on the North Downs
Mountain Biking on the South Downs

For full information on all our
guides, books and eBooks,
visit our website:
**www.cicerone.co.uk**